Essential OpenDoc

Essential OpenDoc®

Cross-Platform Development for OS/2®, Macintosh®, and Windows® Programmers

Jesse Feiler and Anthony Meadow

Addison-Wesley Developers Press

Reading, Massachusetts • Menlo Park, California • New York
Don Mills, Ontario • Wokingham, England • Amsterdam
Bonn • Sydney • Singapore • Tokyo • Madrid • San Juan
Paris • Seoul • Milan • Mexico City • Taipei

Many of the designations used by manufacturers and sellers to distinguish their products are claimed as trademarks. Where those designations appear in this book, and Addison-Wesley was aware of a trademark claim, the designations have been printed in initial capital letters or all capital letters.

The authors and publisher have taken care in preparation of this book, but make no expressed or implied warranty of any kind and assume no responsibility for errors or omissions. No liability is assumed for incidental or consequential damages in connection with or arising out of the use of the information or programs contained herein.

Library of Congress Cataloging-in-Publication Data

Feiler, Jesse.
    Essential OpenDoc : cross-platform development for OS/2,
Macintosh, and Windows programmers / Jesse Feiler and Anthony
Meadow.
        p.   cm.
    Includes index.
    ISBN 0-201-47958-3
    1. Cross-platform software development. 2. Microcomputers-
-Programming.   I. Meadow, Anthony.   II. Title.
QA76.76.D47M43   1996   95-44150
                                                             CIP

A-W Developers Press is a division of Addison-Wesley Publishing Company.

Sponsoring Editors: Keith Wollman and Martha Steffen
Project Manager: Sarah Weaver
Production Coordinator: Erin Sweeney
Cover design: Ann Gallager
Text design: Andrew T. Wilson
Set in 11 point New Century Schoolbook by Carpenter Graphics

1 2 3 4 5 6 7 8 9 -MA- 0099989796
First printing, February, 1996

Addison-Wesley books are available for bulk purchases by corporations, institutions, and other organizations. For more information please contact the Corporate, Government, and Special Sales Department at (800) 238-9682.

Find A-W Developers Press on the World-Wide Web at:
http://www.aw.com/devpress/

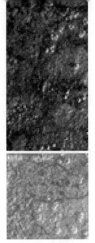

Contents

Preface

The OpenDoc development partners are committed to making OpenDoc as widely available as possible. OpenDoc itself, together with significant documentation and examples, is available from a number of Internet sites, which are listed in the Appendix. Additionally, CD-ROMs with that material and more are distributed to developers associated with these partners. You should not have any difficulty finding OpenDoc; if you do, contact one of the sources listed in the Appendix. The versions of OpenDoc and its examples available on the Internet or on developer CD-ROMs are updated frequently.

OpenDoc Versions and This Book

Typically, software has been developed in a process that sees one or more "alpha" versions of the software released for testing, followed by one or more "beta" versions. In the case of development tools, the interfaces are normally frozen in the beta versions, as is the functionality. Because of the complexity of OpenDoc itself as well as the difficulty of coordinating multi-platform development, OpenDoc has been released during development in a different manner. "Development releases" which did not have to adhere to corporate standards for alpha and beta quality software were released as soon as possible to a wide range of developers. Open-Doc and its interfaces changed significantly between these releases. When Apple released OpenDoc 1.0 for the Mac OS in late 1995, it followed the release of DR3; DR4, which was released at the beginning of 1996, contained the final OpenDoc 1.0 software, together with tools, examples, and documentation that facilitated its use. The Windows and OS/2 versions of Open-Doc 1.0 were still under development by IBM at that time.

The code samples and screenshots in this book are mostly drawn from Apple's DR3 and DR4 releases, since they were the most complete at the time of writing.

Acknowledgments

OpenDoc is about collaboration; so is this book. It could never have been written without tremendous and generous assistance from many people. Those listed here are only the tip of the iceberg. Their help and encouragement has made writing the book a manageable task.

At Addison-Wesley, Keith Wollman (sponsoring editor) and Sarah Weaver (production manager) were always available, always helpful, and immensely encouraging. When we backed ourselves into verbal corners, Sarah was particularly helpful. Martha Steffen's initial support of the project, followed by Keith's continuing help and advice on the presentation of the material helped focus the book.

Jim Black, one of Apple's OpenDoc evangelists, has been a stalwart bastion of assistance. Without him, this book would not have been written. Shaan Pruden, another evangelist at Apple, was also tremendously helpful, providing the jumping-off point for a major section of the book.

At Bear River Associates, Eric Wong labored long and hard to provide a number of the illustrations in this book. We wanted to use actual screenshots of OpenDoc software rather than artists' renderings. This meant that someone (and it was Eric) had to coax pre-alpha software to work sufficiently to be able to capture it in a PICT file.

Also at Apple, Vincent Lo from the OpenDoc development team provided invaluable comments and notes on the technical aspects of OpenDoc. His contribution clarified our understanding of OpenDoc and helped make the technical chapters more accurate and complete.

At IBM, Scott Hebner was of great assistance and support in this project.

Bob Beech, President and CEO of Pharos Technologies, Inc., graciously allowed us to reprint his white paper as Chapter 13 of this book.

We would also like to thank the many members of the OpenDoc teams at IBM, Novell, and Apple for their assistance.

Finally, Carole McClendon of Waterside Productions was instrumental in seeing the project through to fruition.

These people have all contributed immensely to this book, and we thank them profusely. They have helped make the book better than it otherwise would have been. At the same time, we must point out that if errors do exist, they are there despite this assistance and must be laid at the authors' doorsteps.

Writing a book almost always means taking some personal time to do the writing. Tony would like to thank Diana, Jeremy, and Erica for their patience and support while he was working on this book. If Anni, Blanche, and Ernest had in any way contributed to the development of this book, Jesse would certainly express profound thanks; they didn't, and he won't.

About this Book

This book is about OpenDoc—what it is and how to use it. Is it possible that it really is the breakthrough in ease of use that its proponents claim? Are we truly at a point when people can use computers with much less training than they have needed heretofore? The answer may very well be yes, and not for reasons of hype. OpenDoc addresses profound issues regarding how computer software is developed and how people use computers.

OpenDoc is a new way of creating and working with computer software. In this book, you will see how it evolved and the promise that it holds. Developers, users, systems integrators, consultants, solution providers, and managers all face the challenge of learning this new environment: what it is, how to use it, and how to recognize when OpenDoc is the appropriate solution to a given problem. This book provides the essential introduction to OpenDoc for these people. A few terms used in this book might be new to you—not the least of which is OpenDoc. The following excerpt from the CI Labs home page (www.cilabs.org) defines two of them:

> Component Integration Laboratories, Inc. (CI Labs) is a nonprofit organization founded by Apple Computer, Inc.; IBM Corporation; and Novell Inc. CI Labs provides the technological specifications and foundation technology for developing and integrating component software through the OpenDoc component software architecture.

OpenDoc is the cross-platform, component software architecture that interoperates on:

Windows 95, NT and 3.x

Mac OS

OS/2

AIX

OpenDoc component software architecture provides software integration that enables distributed, cross-platform component software and brings a new level of computing power to users.

OpenDoc is an object-oriented technology. If you are not familiar with the basics of object-oriented design, you might want to read one of the many books or articles on the topic. (A detailed knowledge is not required to understand the basics of OpenDoc.)

Most development today is being undertaken using frameworks and C or C++ as a programming language. In recognition of this, the code examples in this book are mostly C++; however, you can write code for the OpenDoc architecture using other languages— even non-object-oriented ones. The framework of choice for use with OpenDoc is ODF—the OpenDoc Development Framework. It is discussed in Chapter 16, and examples are given in several places in the book.

OpenDoc 1.0 for the Macintosh was released in November 1995. The Windows and OS/2 implementations ran a few months behind. Since the Macintosh version was more complete, most of the screen shots and code samples in this book are derived from the OpenDoc DR3 release for the Macintosh. Rest assured that the code and part behavior on the other platforms as well as on the final OpenDoc release are very close to what is presented here.

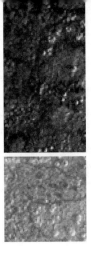

Introduction

OpenDoc has a distinguished technological heritage. It addresses issues of system design and computer interface strategy that are complex and far from trivial. However, two fundamental human principles underlie OpenDoc and its design:

1. **People like to put things together.** Tools and ideas have been combined and recombined throughout human history, with new combinations often accounting for what we call "progress."

2. **People use tools constantly**, and they want to have the right tool for the job.

Until OpenDoc, both of these very human desires were hard to accomplish with the computers and software that were widely available. In some senses, the first fifty years of the computer age can be characterized as consisting of repeated (and usually unsuccessful) attempts to combine and share data among different applications as well as attempts to get individual applications to work together successfully.

Putting Things Together

People put things together. People like to put things together. Putting things together is arguably one of the activities that defines human beings. Although scientists have observed some other animals using tools (an activity once thought to be uniquely human) the constant combination and synthesis of tools and ideas does seem to be a purely human activity. And it is one that accounts for much of the life we take for granted. Inasmuch as tools and ideas can represent parts of our history, their use and reuse can combine and synthesize disparate parts of the human experience into new, interesting, and useful tools and ideas.

Putting Things Together: Deliberately versus Experimentally

This very human activity of putting things together happens in two ways. First, people can, after some thought, put things together in a planned way for a specific purpose—in a **deliberate** manner. Sometimes this represents years and years of work by many people; in other cases it represents a "Eureka!" experience by an individual. Second, people can combine tools and ideas with no planned outcome anticipated, in order to see what will happen— in an **experimental** manner. These activities are a constant part of our daily lives, from toddlers assembling mysterious structures of blocks, to scientists doing "pure" research in laboratories, to amateur matchmakers arranging a dinner party to bring two people together.

Putting Things Together: Combination versus Synthesis

When things are brought together, they may retain their own characteristics in a **combination**; for example, the components of a sundae or a clock radio are recognizable in the resulting product. However, once components are brought together in a **synthesis**, they may not be recognizable. For example, flour, water, salt, and yeast individually bear no resemblance in taste or texture to the loaf of bread that results when they are combined.

In putting things together, people make little distinction between tools, ideas, and physical objects. This can reach farcical depths as in Hollywood "concept" movies that combine the latest fads and stars with last year's smash box office concept movie.

Putting things together does not always result in a larger or more complicated entity than the sum of its components. In some cases, the result is simpler to use or conceptualize. Both a Grand Marnier souffle and the City of New York are syntheses of many components and ingredients. In their synthesized forms, they are easier to identify and to talk about.

Putting Things Together: Planning

Because putting things together is an important activity for humans, designers of tools, objects, and ideas often plan ahead to allow these things to be combined. There are three ways to do this:

1. Complete closed design
2. Particular closed design
3. Open design

Complete Closed Design

In a **complete closed design**, the designer plans for all possible combinations and syntheses. This type of design is exemplified by vacuum cleaners and blenders that take a wide range of attachments—but only from their own manufacturers. It can also be seen in the planned cities designed and sometimes built from the late 1800s until the mid-twentieth century. The advantages of this design are a consistency and completeness, but its drawbacks are precisely the same. (The consistency of the terraced houses in a suburban tract may be mind-numbingly boring to some.) Furthermore, the completeness of the design—whether it be a city or a kitchen appliance—depends on the imagination of the planners.

Particular Closed Design

In a **particular closed design**, no plans for combination and synthesis are made. Cities with no zoning ordinances and single-purpose hand tools are examples of this approach. Whatever happens will happen, often at the cost of duplication of effort and often resulting in a chaotic appearance. On the other hand, this duplication and chaos may provide a vital synergistic environment of constantly evolving tools, ideas, and objects.

Open Design

The third approach—**open design**—calls for standards and guidelines for putting things together. Zoning codes for cities are examples of this approach as are quarter-inch chucks that are a standard for drill bits and other attachments. Standards and guidelines may be **planned** (e.g., zoning) or **evolutionary** (e.g., the standard for drill bits in the United States).

So much of our daily lives (not to mention the progress of the human race) depends on combinations and syntheses, so it stands to reason that those tools, objects, and ideas that can most readily be put together are usually the most valuable. Even when it is difficult to put things together, people will often find a way to do so because of the benefits they derive from the result. For example, note the jury-rigged contraptions people create in their work areas. Combinations of fans, chairs, cartons, and books are arranged for comfort, convenience, and aesthetics, often to the amazement of people not involved in the creation of the working "nest."

Putting Things Together: OpenDoc

Considering the human passion for putting things together and the usefulness of the results of these combinations and syntheses, it is not surprising that from the beginning of the computer age people have tried to combine computers, application programs, and data. In putting them together, the points raised earlier have all been seen:

- Putting things together is something people do and like to do and can provide benefits and progress.
- Putting things together can be done *deliberately* for a specific purpose or *experimentally* to see what will happen as a result.
- Putting things together may result in a *combination*, in which the components are recognizable, or in a *synthesis*, in which they are not.
- Putting things together does not require any limitations. Tools, ideas, and physical objects can be combined with themselves and with each other.

- Putting things together is facilitated (or hindered) by the design used to do so: *complete closed, particular closed,* and *open* designs.
- Putting things together in an open design depends on standards and guidelines, which may be *planned* or which may be *evolutionary*.

Using this terminology, one could say that OpenDoc technology is an open design for putting things together based on standards that have been developed by its designers from Apple, IBM, Novell, and CI Labs. OpenDoc supports both combinations and syntheses and allows you to combine tools as well as ideas. Most important, however, OpenDoc provides a method for performing this most basic and important of human activities: putting things together.

Finding the Right Tool for the Job

The proliferation of tools (application programs) on an individual's personal computer parallels the proliferation of tools in a kitchen drawer or on a workshop toolbench. The do-it-yourselfer knows the frustration of searching for a wrench to tighten a nut or bolt only to find that of the half dozen or so wrenches available, not a single one is the right size. The amateur baker has a similar experience (and frustration) searching for the size and shape baking pan called for in a given recipe from among the clutter of pans in the cupboard.

The accumulation of nearly identical tools not only takes up space. It also poses problems for the user when those nearly identical tools function in dissimilar ways. While the example of resetting electric clocks after a power failure is hoary with over-use, the fact that manufacturers of these clocks still have not managed to provide a consistent way of setting them keeps the example alive. The householder recovering from a power failure may easily have a dozen or so clocks to reset. The task is complicated by the inconsistency in the ways in which these clocks are set.

These situations are familiar enough that it is not surprising to find them repeated on personal computers. The proliferation of similar but different tools and the problem of similar tools behaving differently are inevitable by-products of the development of better tools, each of which is more appropriate for a specific task and each of which boasts an improved way of using the tool. (Sometimes the improvement in a new tool is that it is less expensive than its predecessors. A tradeoff has been made in which the new tool is an improvement over its predecessors not from a functional point of view, but merely from an economic point of view.)

Standardizing Tools and Tasks

Developers as well as users of tools periodically strive to make order out of this disarray. Sometimes order is achieved by the development of standards—either formal or informal. For example, in the United States, standard window sizes have evolved, thereby allowing people to buy curtains and window shades from stock rather than having them custom-made. This benefits everyone—builders, decorators, and consumers. The disadvantage is that as windows and their furnishings increasingly are manufactured in a relatively few standard sizes, architects and consumers who want a nonstandard window size (or shape) must either compromise on their design or pay higher prices.

Using Adjustable, Multipurpose Tools

In other cases, many different tools can be replaced with a single adjustable, multipurpose tool. The adjustable wrench is an example. However, as with the use of standards to limit the proliferation of tools, there are disadvantages to a single, adjustable tool. Such a tool may be more expensive than many single-purpose tools combined. Also, it may be a "Jack-of-all-trades, master-of-none" compromise.

Using the Right Tool for the Task with OpenDoc

Most people find that for tasks they care about, there is no substitute for the right tool. Sometimes it is necessary to compromise—either use a tool that isn't exactly right or adhere to standard dimensions and requirements that don't reflect what you want to do. (Lawnmowers are not successfully put together with socket wrenches of the wrong size.) It is for situations like this that many people have one (or more!) sets of perhaps a dozen or so wrenches.

While the problems of having many different physical tools involve a lack of space and the need for organization, the problems of having many different tools on a computer are very different. The computer easily handles the storing of different tools—the price of storage has drastically declined over the years. Computers also are very good at organizing things and presenting them appropriately.

The difficulty with using multiple tools (application programs) on a computer is that historically they have not worked well together. The output from one often cannot be used as the input to another—sometimes even when both are provided by the same developer! In some ways, the obstacle to finding and using the right software tool for the job is simply the difficulty of putting things together on the computer.

Summary

Fifty years into the computer age, we have spent enough time playing with the new toys and tools, and we have learned minutiae about computers and application programs that we never should have had to. (There is nothing wrong with this: Each new technology starts by making demands on its users that are excessive. The maturity of a technology—and its widespread use—comes only when these trivia are hidden from view.) The technology of OpenDoc—and the motives that drive its development—have their roots equally in today's real-world computing and in the age-old human drive to put things together.

In this book, you will see how OpenDoc works and how to use it. Of necessity much of the book describes the evolutionary process of moving from your current computing environment to one that is fundamentally different. You should bear in mind, however, that the new environment is in many ways radically different from the old, since its focus is on the quintessentially human and critically important task of putting things together.

Part I

Invitation to OpenDoc

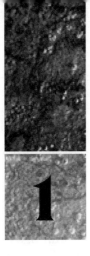

Where We Are and How We Got Here

The Computer Age is very young—about 50 years old, depending on when you place its birth. In the mid-1940s, precursors to modern-day computers existed although you would not have likely found a machine that would clearly be comparable to what we call a computer. By the early 1950s, however, several electronic brains existed that can be recognized as what we today call a computer.

The history of the Computer Age is a fascinating (and remarkably neglected) subject. As in any field where history is not studied, contemporary practitioners continually struggle to reinvent wheels that were spinning decades before. On the rare occasions when they delve into old files and newspapers, they are amazed to discover how "advanced" their predecessors were. This chapter cannot begin to cover the vast realm of material, but here you will see that the strands that make up OpenDoc have existed from the dawn of the Computer Age. You will also see why those strands have not been knitted together until now.

The Promise of OpenDoc

According to the developers of OpenDoc (or at least their publicists), "OpenDoc is a revolutionary technology that brings a new class of applications and documents to the Windows, Macintosh, OS/2, UNIX, and other personal-computer platforms. With Open-Doc, hardware and software developers can deliver new software technologies to individual users, better server integration to corporate users, and enhanced multimedia content to all users."

These promises have been made before (which, if nothing else, indicates that they matter to people). There is reason to believe that OpenDoc will fulfill these promises and the great expectations that accompany it. Not only is it a powerful, fully-thought-out architecture, but it also is a mature technology. Its maturity comes in large part from its sturdy underpinnings (such as OSA and SOM), which have been incorporated after proving themselves in other environments. The maturity also arises from the fact that OpenDoc and its developers recognize and appreciate—and deal with—the problems that have hobbled other promising technologies. The world will not suddenly change to an OpenDoc world overnight. Even as OpenDoc matures and evolves, it will coexist with other technologies and architectures. Change and interoperability are constants in the world of computers.

The History of the Contemporary Computer Age

To put the promise of OpenDoc in perspective, it is instructive to look at the history of the contemporary Computer Age. (There have arguably been other computer ages, notably during the Industrial Revolution and possibly in the mists of antiquity in Greece, Egypt, and Babylon.) This history is incomplete, but it is useful to consider the following five eras of the Computer Age:

1. The Dawn: Before 1955
2. The Mainframe Era: Mid-1950s to Mid-1960s
3. The Time-sharing Era: Mid-1960s to the Present
4. The Personal Computer Era: 1980 to the Early 1990s
5. The Late 1990s

The Dawn: Before 1955

Computers were developed as computational engines to produce mathematical tables and solve mathematical problems. They were big, expensive, and hard to use. They were also very fast—

that is, compared to the speed of individuals performing the same calculations. Of course, once these calculations had all been performed, periodic updatings might be required. But it appeared the nation's need for these computational engines would be satisfied by a few of them—perhaps a half dozen, perhaps twenty—located at major universities and research centers. After all, how many sine tables do you need?

For this role, the big, expensive, hard-to-use, and relatively scarce computers were fine. They could compute a sine table in three shakes of a lamb's tail. And when errors were found, they could recompute that sine table like greased lightning. (And move on to the calculation of the table to convert lightning speeds to lamb's-tail-shaking speeds.)

Mathematicians and engineers (together with their wives and graduate students) were the users of these machines as well as their operators. There were relatively few of them (machines, users, and operators), and all parties simply got on with their work without worrying much about standards or procedures.

The notion that an ordinary person could in any way directly use a computer was ludicrous. But no one told this to the popular press or the entertainment industry. For example, William Marchant's comedy *The Desk Set* (on Broadway with Shirley Booth and on the screen with Katharine Hepburn) featured a computer wheeled into an office to answer any question that might be asked of it. And in the black-and-white television kinescopes and films from the early 1950s, you can see computers that required no special handling—much less rooms with raised floors and dedicated air conditioning—and that responded to spoken requests. News shows and documentaries featured computers performing feats (and stunts) such as predicting weather and elections, matching up eligible suitors ("computer dating" now seems as quaint a practice as "bundling"), and calculating *pi* to an unseemly number of places.

The Computer Age was born with great expectations on all sides. Unfortunately, people outside the small circle of the truly computer literate believed that those expectations had been realized at that time. This gap between potential and reality was not played up in the press; the fantastic promises of the Computer Age made better copy than did the footnote that potential patrons should call back in a few decades. And vendors of hardware and software needed to sell their products in the here-and-now, not in the sweet hereafter. To be certain, many people and organizations needed what the computers of the time could do—limited though that might be in comparison with their potential. It served no one to point out how much of the promise remained unfulfilled.

The Mainframe Era: Mid-1950s to Mid-1960s

The feats and stunts of the early 1950s were performed by monstrous machines attended by specially trained operators and coders (the term "programmer" was not current until the mid-1950s). There were no real computer languages (FORTRAN appeared at the end of 1954, ALGOL in 1958, and COBOL in 1959). Machines were individually built and often included their own unique sets of instructions.

A few people saw that computers could do much more than mathematical calculations. They started to address problems that dealt more with the organization and storage of large amounts of data than with intensive computations. No longer were there only a few powerful computers located at isolated research labs. The idea of other uses for computers began to enter the popular consciousness, and the machines began to be placed in businesses, factories, and government offices.

This expansion of the use of computers led to the development and production of standardized mainframes, which had standardized instruction sets and standardized routines for their operation. It became possible to advertise in the newspaper for a computer operator or even a computer programmer, although in most cases you needed to hire one that had experience with your specific brand of computer.

Like their predecessors, these machines were big and powerful and designed to handle many different functions. In the Mainframe Era, however, users, operators, and coders of the machines were no longer the same people. Only the computer operators and the support staffs had direct access to the computer. Programmers submitted their programs (on punch cards) to the operators, who then put them into the machines. Users sent their computer tapes into Machine Rooms and wheeled away carts full of printouts.

As computers became more powerful, many of the support functions that previously had been done manually were taken over by the computers themselves. The most visible such shift was the widespread use of compilers—programs that generate computer code automatically.

The direct access between user and computer was gone. Gone was not only the direct verbal access between user and computer that had existed only in the imagination, but also the direct access of people setting switches and wiring circuit boards to perform their calculations. In its place were layers of support staff around both computer and user.

The Time-sharing Era: Mid-1960s to the Present

During this era, computers became even more powerful, and when transistors became the core of machines in the 1960s, many manual tasks were automated. As always, prime candidates for automation were aspects of the computer industry itself. The need to physically mount tapes and drop cards in card readers limited the placement of computers and their users. With advances in telecommunications as well as with more-sophisticated operating systems, computers could support users at remote terminals.

In the Mainframe Era, users had had no direct access to the computer. But in the Time-sharing Era, users could directly access the computer over telephone lines and through increasingly sophisticated operating systems that prevented user A from corrupting user B's data and processes. Direct access had been present at the dawn of the Computer Age, at least in everyone's expectations. Promised, but then taken away, now it was back and it proved to be a big hit. Computer terminals began to sprout everywhere—on bank tellers' counters, on airline ticket agents' desks, throughout large corporations and universities. The notion that computer users needed support staffs because they couldn't communicate directly with a computer was laid to rest with sophisticated operating systems. Of course, the computer itself still needed its own support staff. After all, a computer couldn't run itself.

The Personal Computer Era: 1980 to the Early 1990s

The computers of the early 1950s could store 1,000 (1K) characters in memory. The first personal computers in the early 1980s had 16K of memory. Soon, desktop models sported 256K of memory, the same amount in many mainframe computers of the 1960s and 1970s. In 1995, one computer manufacturer shipped computers with 32MB of memory (that's 32,000 × 1K) as a standard configuration. The computer was upgradable to 768MB. Along with this increase in power came a decrease in the size of computers (even personal computers) as well as their cost. (Even in terms of absolute cost—comparing a 1K machine in 1980 with a 32MB machine in 1995—the cost fell. Add in the effects of inflation as well as the increase in the power of the machine and the drop in the cost of computer power is astonishing.)

Where was all this computer power going? What was it being used for? More tasks were automated—again, starting with tasks on the computer itself. The personal computer was made possible not only because the raw power was placed on the user's desk, but also because that power could be used to run more and more sophisticated operating systems that automated many of the tasks of running the computer.

Recall that in the Mainframe Era, computers were surrounded by support staffs, and users were likewise surrounded by support staffs who could talk to their counterparts in the computer area. In the Time-sharing Era, automation drastically reduced user support staffs, thereby allowing users to deal directly with the computer. Nevertheless, that computer—in its own room, with dedicated air conditioning, raised flooring, and special electrical circuits—still had its own dedicated support staff.

In the Personal Computer Era, people once again were able to interact directly with a computer, just as at the dawn of the Computer Age. More powerful automation allowed the computer to run with no special staff, and users often needed no outside support to run their computers. It appears the configuration of people and computers from the beginning of the Computer Age had been rediscovered—forty years later.

But not the promise of ease of use.

The Late 1990s

In an unfortunately recurring circumstance in the computer world, the computer industry discovered that people didn't want to actually *use* computers. People wanted to do what they thought they had been able to do in the early 1950s: Ask a computer a question or tell a computer to do something. All the layers of support—first manual and later automated—had been devised to reach this goal. In this case, the operating systems and programs that were developed to help people use computers became ends in and of themselves. Many people spent a great deal of time and money developing and supporting them, using them, and teaching their use. Educators and pundits stressed the need for "computer literacy." Few people were bold enough to say, "I'm literate in English and horticulture. I just want the computer to tell me when to put out the dahlias, and I have no interest in computer literacy—whatever that is."

Computers—particularly personal computers—are available throughout the world and are common in many countries. Many people are computer literate and do know how to use these machines—even how to program them. It appears that the markets for computer hardware and software *as they are now* may be close to saturation and maturity.

The riches of the Computer Age have been laid out on the banquet table, but a sizable number of people have decided to pass, or to just have the equivalent of "a little soup" ("just word processing"). Fortunately, the power of ever-expanding computers can be used to take one step further—a step that invites the millions of people who don't want to be computer literate to join in the fun.

That step is consistent with those that have been taken throughout the Computer Age: more of computer operations themselves are automated and so became hidden from the user. The user and the task, without intermediation of support staffs, enormous machines, and complex instructions, are the focus of the next era of the Computer Age.

The Evolution of Software Capabilities and Interfaces

While the issues of hardware and system software have been played out, the application software that people use every day has also been evolving. Graphical user interfaces have become more common, and people have quickly adopted them and demanded more from them. As a result, graphical user interfaces, which used to be very simple and intuitive, have become more complex and complicated than anyone ever dreamed.

Basic Word Processing—WYSIWYG

Consider the evolution of basic word processing software. In the early 1980s, it was radical and exciting to see text on the screen much the same way as it would later appear on paper. The addition of interface elements (such as rulers) that recalled everyday physical objects made it seem that the problems of teaching people how to use their computers would be solved. Figure 1-1 shows a simple word processing document window with WYSIWYG (what-you-see-is-what-you-get) text and a ruler that looks much like the mechanical levers on standard typewriters.

People were so excited by this new technology that they immediately began asking for more. In particular, they wanted to be able to have two or more document windows open simultaneously (see Figure 1-2).

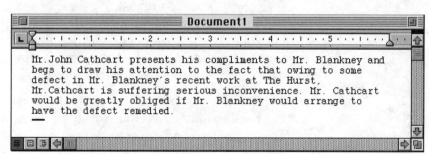

Figure 1-1.

A simple word processing document window

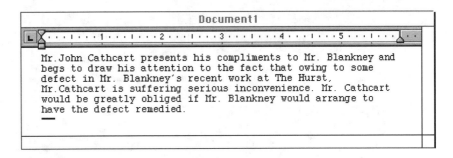

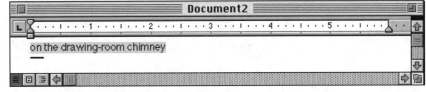

Figure 1-2.

Two word processing document windows

It is worth pausing to consider how momentous this concept was. It recognized the fact that people might actually want to work on two things at the same time. This notion, although commonplace, was a radical departure for software designers in the early 1980s. Even today, some application programs still assume their users will work on only one document at a time.

Cut-Copy-Paste

Once people could work on two documents, there were occasions when it would be useful to move text from one document to another (see Figure 1-3).

The ability to copy data within and among applications was one of the most attractive features of the first Macintosh computers. For this to work, a few very basic types of data that many applications would recognize had to be defined. Fortunately, this task was simple, since all data on personal computers at that time consisted either of text or of spreadsheets. The emergence of the Macintosh in 1984 added a third standard data type—images.

Over time, as new features were added to applications, users were happy to be able to do even more with their computers. For example, they could modify text by underlining or italicizing it, as shown in Figure 1-4.

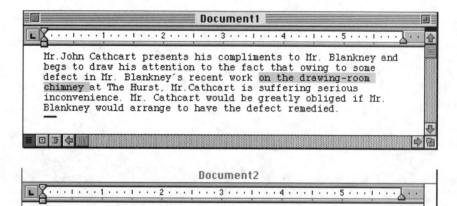

Figure 1-3.

Text pasted from one window to another

The combination of styled text with standard cutting and pasting immediately caused problems. Users expected to be able to paste styled text just as they had done with unstyled text, in the manner shown in Figure 1-5. While this usually worked within a given application, copying text with such style information between applications was a problem. Styled text was not one of the basic data types, and each application had to decide on how to add the styling information to the basic text. Although (conflicting) standards quickly emerged, the simple task of pasting styled

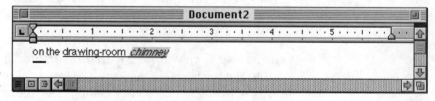

Figure 1-4.

Styled text

text is a problem that has not been totally resolved even today. It is not clear, for example, whether the user whose work is shown in Figure 1-5 truly intended the font from Document 2 to be pasted into Document 1. Certainly the words were intended to be pasted, and quite possibly the emphasis provided by the italics and underlining were meant to be copied. But would most users have wanted to carry the font from Document 2 into Document 1?

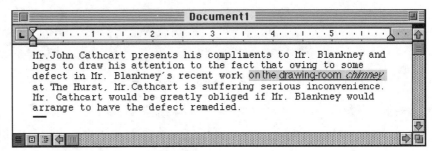

Figure 1-5.

Styled text pasted from one window to another

Mixing Data Types

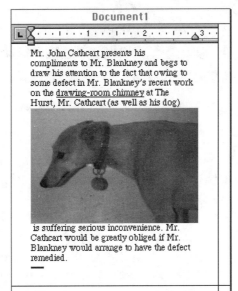

Figure 1-6.

An image pasted into a word processing document

In the original world of personal computers—where everything was divided into text, spreadsheet, or graphics applications—cutting and pasting was straightforward. You copied text from a text application into another text application, graphics from a graphics application to another graphics application, and so on. Soon, however, people began to think these boundaries were too arbitrary. It didn't seem far-fetched to want to merge the data types, as shown in Figure 1-6.

Interfaces—Power versus Complexity

Once again, as the technology advanced new issues arose. Figure 1-7 shows the user interface of the word processing application (Microsoft Word) used in the previous illustrations. The Toolbars across the top of the screen contain many valuable features and functions, while the Status bar at the bottom provides information about the document and its environment.

Figure 1-7.

A word processing window shown with its interface (Microsoft Word)

Despite the many buttons, none allow the user to edit the picture that has just been pasted into the document. This is not surprising, since word processing applications are designed to handle primarily text. Most handle the issue of editing graphics by using a variation of the interface shown in Figure 1-8.

When you double-click on the image, a copy of it is opened in its own editing window and the graphics Toolbar is placed across the bottom of the screen above the Status bar. Study Figure 1-8 for a moment, and think about what it shows. The word processing Toolbar contains more than three dozen buttons; the graphics Toolbar has a more modest two dozen. Each window has nearly a dozen controls of its own. This is power, this is flexibility—and this is potentially confusing.

Furthermore, the program remains a word processing application. Its graphics capabilities are significant, but they are quite limited when compared to a dedicated graphics application.

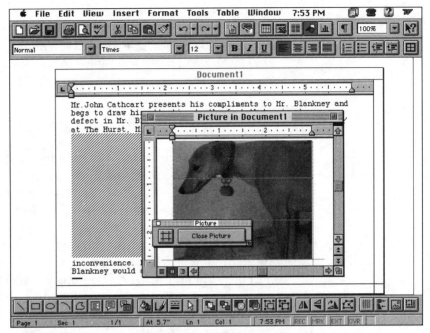

Figure 1-8.

The image editing window and its interface (Microsoft Word)

Note that Microsoft Word is shown as an example because of its widespread use on many personal computer platforms. It is neither the best nor the worst when it comes to interface and functionality. Most word processing applications today have comparable interfaces and functionality.

As you can see, in this evolutionary process a simple, intuitive interface with a simple window in which you can type text as you'll see it when it's printed out has become over time a powerful application that is no longer so simple and intuitive. Each additional feature and piece of complexity is justified, but the result is not necessarily a product that is easier to use than the simple word processing program from which it descended.

An example of this is the advent of desktop video. It took several years, but eventually all the major business productivity applications (word processors, spreadsheets, databases, and so on) incorporated new code and interface elements to allow copying, pasting, and basic editing of video. This was great if you wanted to write a memo and include a video clip showing how to change the toner cartridge in a photocopy machine. But the extra baggage was also passed on to people who wanted only to type a letter.

The OpenDoc Approach

OpenDoc represents a new way of addressing these issues. It doesn't add endless features to monster-sized applications ("monster apps") so that they can do more and more things to more and more types of data. Instead, think of OpenDoc as a simple document that is designed to let you drop things into it. Unlike with traditional applications, the containing document and its implementing code don't pretend to know how to edit their embedded data. When you paste underlined text into a traditional word processing document, the word processing program must be capable not only of underlining text (not all word processors can!), but also of understanding how your program has encoded the underlining. OpenDoc provides an environment in which the interface and functionality of data move with it as it is dropped into other documents.

In breaking apart monster apps into pieces that are relevant to the given task and its data, OpenDoc helps to simplify the user interface (not to mention the executing code). Once again, simplification moves the user close to the task and makes the software less obtrusive. The user who wants to set up a database of recipes may well be confused or irritated by the video editing tools that are provided for the Little League coach who wants to set up a database of highlights from season games. The close connection of data, interface, and functionality implies that they don't spill over into other domains of documents; you don't see a slide into third when you're deep into the intricacies of strudel, and you don't see the editing tools you'd need to use either.

With OpenDoc, there's less software on the screen at any given time, and what there is, is more likely to be relevant—and necessary—to the task at hand.

The Road Ahead

In the early 1990s, the Apple/Motorola/IBM PowerPC chip and the Intel Pentium chip brought a new shot of brawn to the desktop. Consumers happily snapped up machines that ran twice—or ten—times faster than previous machines. These people didn't type two or ten times faster and they didn't create spreadsheets two or ten times bigger. . . and had they wanted to, they couldn't have. As always, the systems engineers took a big chunk of processing power off the top. This processing power was used to make operating systems more powerful and intuitive, to make communications, speech synthesis, and desktop video usable realities—and to change the way in which people use computers.

To think of OpenDoc as the end of software is a slight exaggeration. But in the context of those millions of people who either don't use computers or use them minimally, the prospect of doing work without worrying about the computer, operating system, program, or software is inviting enough to encourage many of them to join in.

In short, OpenDoc can help users realize those expectations raised more than forty years ago when people first began to think about computers. It is not an answer to last year's problem, or an easier way to run the previous year's "killer app." It is, indeed, what people have been waiting for—and what many customers were disappointed to find out they *didn't* have.

In Part I of this book, you will read about the basic OpenDoc concepts (Chapter 2), what OpenDoc means to computer users (Chapter 3), and what it means to developers, manufacturers, and system integrators (Chapter 4).

Part II takes an in-depth look at the technical issues of OpenDoc. Parts III and IV deal with the transition to OpenDoc and the development of OpenDoc software and solutions.

Basic OpenDoc Concepts

2

All technical books suffer from the chicken-and-the-egg syndrome. That is, if the terms and concepts are defined first, their purposes and uses may be mysterious. If the purposes and objective of the technology are defined first, terms need to be introduced helter-skelter (or in dreaded footnotes) or else the user will be lost.

This chapter briefly covers the basic OpenDoc terminology and concepts. Subsequent chapters show how those concepts are used and refines the definitions of the terms. Read this chapter to get a basic familiarity with the terminology and then move on to Chapter 3, "What Is OpenDoc? The User's Answer," to see how they are used in real life.

Why OpenDoc?

In the Introduction, you saw how OpenDoc arose from the basic human ways of working with tools and tasks. In Chapter 1, you saw how it evolved from the history of the Computer Age because people want to directly deal with their work without the intermediation of support staffs and complicating layers of applications and operating systems. In this chapter, a third force motivating the development of OpenDoc is revealed: Developers of software are close to a crisis point.

Old-timers in the personal computer world smile fondly when remembering the days when a single floppy disk contained enough space for an operating system, a word processing program, and a good-sized document. Such a word processing program could be written by an individual in a few months' time while holding down a respectable full-time job. This is no longer the case.

Programs are becoming laden with more and more features. This is as a direct result of the fact that people do not know how to evaluate software. If word processor X has 492 features and word processor Y has 503 features, they believe Y is the one to get. Evaluating the quality and usefulness of the features seems to be beyond the ken of the buyer. (Educators and authors who expound "computer literacy" certainly don't help the situation. Instead of teaching nonprogrammers how to program, they should be concentrating on teaching them how to evaluate soft-ware. This would eliminate "feature creep" in one fell swoop. But it apparently is too late to do this.)

As programs get more complex, more time is required to test, debug, and then revise them. What can take months to write can take several years to test, debug, and revise.

Just as structured programming offered some relief to the tremendous programming backlog of the 1970s and early 1980s, object-oriented programming did the same for beleaguered devel-opers in the late 1980s and early 1990s. But it was not enough. This incremental change did nothing to make the development, testing, and modification of software easier. A new way of work-ing was needed.

Further, users found it expensive to cope with enhancements and revisions to software and operating systems. A small office of half a dozen people could easily keep one person busy full time man-aging them: testing them to ensure everything still ran, critical documents still looked the same, and the numbers in spread-sheets were correct.

Recall that OpenDoc starts from the premise that people will combine their tools in idiosyncratic and unpredictable ways to solve their own problems. Further, it starts from the assumption that people want to deal directly with their tasks, without visible intermediation. And finally, it starts as well from the notion that no version of a software product is final (although manufacturers are hesitant to stress this point). The fact is, hardware and software are always evolving. You will always be upgrading something or other. The model should not be of a stable environment that is destabilized periodically (weekly, it seems!) by a new version of an operating system, application, printer driver, or server. Instead, the model should be of a stable environment that is *not* destabilized as new operating systems, applications, printer drivers, or servers are installed.

Why not have an environment that respects the way in which people work, minimizes the visibility of the computer, and accepts the fact that change is a constant part of this world?

Why not have OpenDoc?

Basic OpenDoc Concepts

A primary goal of OpenDoc is to provide a simpler yet more powerful interface for the user to work with. Not surprisingly, from the user's point of view there are only five basic concepts to think about—and these concepts are remarkably simple:

- Documents
- Parts
- Containers
- Components
- Stationery

Each of these concepts is addressed in the following sections.

Documents: Metaphor and Container

So far, OpenDoc has been sketched in broad humanistic and behavioral strokes. Now it's time for terminology and a bit of computerese. It's all very well to talk about tools and tasks, but exactly what do you see on the computer screen? What are you going to use? In the next chapter, you'll see how to use OpenDoc; here, the basic concepts are defined.

Central to OpenDoc is the concept of a document. The document is a basic metaphor of graphical user interfaces. That is, most applications, when launched, present a document image to the user, ready for data to be entered. The document may be a blank letter or spreadsheet, but it is part of the visual metaphor intrinsic to the graphical user interface in which you take a document out of a folder, lay it on your desktop, and start to work on it.

The document metaphor is valid for many applications—for example, desktop publishing and word processing are designed in most cases to create physical documents. It is not so obvious in some other applications, such as telecommunications software, disk utilities, or databases, where sometimes the metaphor is stretched to force a "document" to be something other than what a paper document would be. In still other cases, the document metaphor is conveniently dropped.

In OpenDoc, the task you are doing is the center of attention, and the document is the physical representation of that task. Often the document is analogous to a paper document, in other cases it is a more abstract metaphor; in all cases, however, when you start to do something using OpenDoc technology, you either create or open a document. When you are finished doing your task, you close the document.

This document metaphor is more powerful than the original paper metaphor is. The OpenDoc document is the physical representation of the task and is the container of all of its data. OpenDoc controls how documents contain things, and it does this in a very specific way (see the section, "Containers," later in this chapter). In fact, OpenDoc can be viewed as a way of coordinating and managing the parts of a document, where those parts may be much richer and more complex than the sentences in a paragraph.

Parts: Pieces of Documents

Traditional documents—both paper and those created by programs that rely on graphical user interfaces—usually are relatively unstructured. Where a structure is enforced, it often is imposed superficially on the document. (For all the apparent orderliness of a spreadsheet, in many cases if you could see how the actual data storage is arranged, you would be taken aback.)

Parts of documents in an OpenDoc world are very structured objects that obey very specific rules. They are, indeed, objects in the sense of objects in an object-oriented world. They represent data and the computer code needed to manipulate that data.

What Parts Can Do

The code for OpenDoc parts generally should be able to do the following basic tasks:

- Initialize the part—allocate and prepare its memory structures.
- Open the part—read its data in from storage.
- Draw the contents.
- Handle events such as mouse clicks, menu selections.
- Write the part to storage.

Most parts are developed with frameworks (such as the OpenDoc Development Framework). These frameworks provide standard code for these tasks. Some of these tasks are generic. For example, events are handled pretty much the same way for most parts. Other tasks—such as drawing, reading, and writing—are routine but must be customized for each part. In all cases, basic OpenDoc part functionality can be provided by the framework so that only the part-specific tasks need to be designed and written.

If you examine the previous list of tasks which parts should be able to perform, you will see that these are basic tasks you would expect most programmatic objects to be able to perform. Programmers are not being asked to do things that are unusual in the context of traditional programs. They are being asked *not* to worry about certain more global concerns, for example, the creation and allocation of permanent storage and deciding how to dispatch events (i.e., which part gets the mouse click). Open-Doc parts live in very small worlds of their own, albeit circumscribed and predictable worlds. From the standpoints of users and programmers, this makes developing, using, and combining OpenDoc parts easy to do. The baggage of the monster app's overhead is gone, replaced by an elegant, standardized, and powerful mechanism deep in the heart of the OpenDoc world that handles common functionality and asks part editors only to do what they must.

Identifying Parts

For OpenDoc to manage parts properly, each part is identified in two ways: by kind and by category.

A part's **kind** is similar to a file type. It identifies the format of its stored data. Part kinds are null-terminated 7-bit ASCII ISO strings that identify the editor that created or last managed it in as descriptive a way as possible ("BearRiver:onlineService" or "PhilmontSoftwareMill:multimediaController" are examples). These strings are internal to OpenDoc; more meaningful strings are shown to the users.

While the part kind suggests a part editor that can be used for a part, many parts contain standard types of data that may possibly be edited by editors other than the one that created or last managed it. The part **category** is a standardized ISO string, coordinated by CI Labs, that identifies categories of parts such as text, movies, bitmaps, styled text, and database.

OpenDoc binds the appropriate editor to each part as needed, usually based on its previous experience with the part in question. However, users have the opportunity to exercise greater control over which editors to use for which parts. In Figure 2-1, the OpenDoc Editor Setup window is shown.

The window reflects the state of OpenDoc's internal database and shows the kinds of OpenDoc parts that are located on this particular computer, the categories into which they fall, and the preferred editor for each part. If the user wishes to change the default editor for a particular kind of part, clicking on the Choose Editor... button will bring up the dialog shown in Figure 2-2.

OpenDoc presents the part editors that can possibly handle the selected part kind; the user can then choose which one to use as a default for that kind of part. Of course, there are times when a user might want to use a different part editor. If this is to be a

Editor Setup		
Kind	Category	Editor
DrawEditor	2DGraphics	DrawEditor 1.0
ODF Draw Example	2DGraphics	<unchosen>
Other 2DGraphics	2DGraphics	DrawEditor 1.0
ODF Bitmap Example	Bitmap	<unchosen>
Picture data	Bitmap	PictureViewer 1.0
Picture file	Bitmap	<unchosen>
Other Bitmap	Bitmap	<unchosen>
ODF Button Example	Control	ODFButton 1.0d11
Other Control	Control	<unchosen>
ODF Nothing Example	ODF Example	<unchosen>

Choose Editor...

Figure 2-1.
OpenDoc Editor Setup window

permanent replacement (for example switching from text editing part editor A to text editing part editor B), it can be done in the Preferred Editor dialog. On the other hand, if this choice is applicable only to a particular part in a certain document, the user can open the Document Info or Part Info dialog from inside any OpenDoc document and select the preferred editor there. Figure 2-3 shows the Document Info dialog. (The Part Info dialog is similar, but allows the user to specify the name, kind, and editor of a selected part rather than for the root part of the document.)

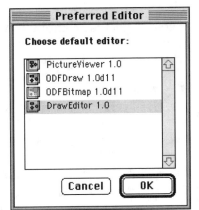

Preferred Editor

Choose default editor:

- PictureViewer 1.0
- ODFDraw 1.0d11
- ODFBitmap 1.0d11
- DrawEditor 1.0

Cancel   OK

Figure 2-2.
Preferred Editor dialog

Note that OpenDoc provides the ability for users to change the kind of a part dynamically. This is part of the standard OpenDoc interface in the Document Info dialog; it is implemented by individual part editors where it makes sense.

The Best Parts

OpenDoc parts are most useful when they are concentrated on a particular type of data and/or a particular task. Such parts are easily combined and recombined in ways that their authors may

```
┌─────────────────────────────────────────────────┐
│ ▓▓▓▓▓▓▓▓▓▓▓▓▓▓   Document Info   ▓▓▓▓▓▓▓▓▓▓▓▓▓▓ │
│                                                   │
│  ┌──┐      Name:  ┌──────────────────────────┐   │
│  │▦ │             │ ODFTable 1.0d11 1         │   │
│  └──┘   View as: ┌──────────┐  ☐ Bundled      │   │
│                  │ Frame  ▼ │  ☐ Stationery   │   │
│                  └──────────┘  ☐ Show Links   │   │
│                                                   │
│         Category:  Table Container                │
│             Kind: ┌────────────────────────┐ ▼   │
│                   │ ODF Table Example       │     │
│           Editor: ┌────────────────────────┐ ▼   │
│                   │ ODFTable 1.0d11         │     │
│                                                   │
│            Size:  251 bytes on disk               │
│         Created:  Sun, Nov 12, 1995, 2:05 PM      │
│        Modified:  Sun, Nov 12, 1995, 2:07 PM      │
│              By:  Jesse Feiler                    │
│              ID:  65568                            │
│  ┌─────────────────────────────────────────────┐ │
│  │                                               │ │
│  └─────────────────────────────────────────────┘ │
│          ┌────────┐ ┌────────┐ ┌──────────┐      │
│          │ Size...│ │ Cancel │ │    OK    │      │
│          └────────┘ └────────┘ └──────────┘      │
└─────────────────────────────────────────────────┘
```

Figure 2-3.
Document Info dialog

never have dreamed. Parts that become larger, more complicated, and more specific to a particular combination of tasks and data are less easy to reuse.

Containers

Documents contain parts and manage them through basic OpenDoc routines. In fact, OpenDoc's container mechanism is more general than this. OpenDoc parts may themselves contain other parts. They are not required to be able to do this. However, all OpenDoc parts must be able *to be contained* in other parts. OpenDoc documents contain a single root part and any OpenDoc part must be able to be a root part. If that part allows other parts to be contained within it, then the root part (and hence the document) may contain more than one part. It's a simple hierarchical structure.

A part's own data is said to be **intrinsic**. If it contains one or more other parts, those parts contain their own data. When a part is moved into another part, it is said to be **embedded**—its data remains separate from that of the containing part.

The principles of containers, containerization, and embedding of parts are at the core of OpenDoc.

Components

The first three concepts of OpenDoc are straightforward and have parallels in the physical world: Documents contain parts.

Components are pieces of software that act on OpenDoc parts. They can be viewed as the tools that act upon the physical Open-Doc world. There are five primary types of components in the OpenDoc world:

1. Part editors
2. Part viewers
3. Services
4. Extensions
5. Plug-ins

Part Editors

Part editors have been mentioned in the previous section, and you probably have correctly surmised what they are: they are the pieces of code that provide a part's functionality. Much of the editing of an OpenDoc document can be done without involving part editors but many operations do require a part editor's action. For example, the display of a part's content must be handled by the part editor. Also, if alternate types of displays are provided, it is the part editor that manages these displays and draws the appropriate one. Editing that affects that part's content (as opposed to simply adding a part to a document) must be handled by the part editor. Finally, storage (both reading and writing) must be handled by the part editor, in response to a request from the document.

Although conceptually the part editor code is part of the object that also contains the part's data, in reality the part editor is a separate piece of code that is linked in at runtime to the OpenDoc environment. OpenDoc locates the appropriate piece of code by using the part's kind and category.

If a part editor cannot be found for a part in a document, that part cannot be drawn and is shown as a gray image of the appropriate size and shape and at the appropriate location on the screen. It can be manipulated as a part, but its data cannot be touched. Therefore, when it is reopened in an environment that contains the appropriate part editor, its data can be seen and modified.

Whether or not a part editor can be found, users can choose an alternative part editor for a given part.

The days of the floppy disk with the operating system and the (single-file) application are long gone. The monster applications that handle word processing for many people take up 20 to 30 MB of disk space, and their installation process adds hundreds of files to a user's disk. Installation of OpenDoc parts is much simpler, but there nevertheless are usually two files for each type of OpenDoc part that is installed on a machine. One file is the part editor code, and the other is the stationery pad for the part itself (from which you can create OpenDoc documents with a root part of that type). These normally live in separate places on your disk, and you should know where they are. When you clean up your hard disk, leave the directories/folders "Editors" and "Stationery" alone.

Part Viewers

Part viewers are part editors that can only display and print their contents. Developers are encouraged to distribute part viewers with no restriction and to include with them an electronic means of ordering the full part editor. (See Chapter 4, "What Is OpenDoc? The Business Answer" for further discussion of the OpenDoc marketplace.)

Services

Services are software components that do not provide display, storage, or editing functions for parts or documents. They provide other functions for either parts or documents. A spelling service might be available to a document and would examine the text in each part from which it could retrieve text, providing the results to the document (or to the part that initiated the request for the service). Other types of services, among other things, can provide connection to networks and databases and prepare the document and all its parts for a certain type of imaging.

Extensions

OpenDoc extensions allow part editors to communicate with one another. An extension can provide a neutral third party that mediates and manages the requests and communications of two or more parts. They are not visible to the user.

Plug-ins

Plug-ins alter or extend the capabilities of OpenDoc itself. These plug-ins can provide functionality at the document level (and hence to the user when any part in the document is active). Parts need not know about plug-ins, so plug-ins can provide an effective way of extending functionality without affecting individual parts and their editors. (Plug-ins are similar to extensions in the Mac OS.)

Stationery

A user can drag a part into a document (or into another part) and it will be embedded there (the operation can also be done as a cut-and-paste operation). Parts can be marked as **stationery**—that is, when they are dragged into a document (or cut-and-pasted into a document) the original part remains where it was on disk and a new part is incorporated into the document. The metaphor is the straightforward one of a pad of stationery from which you rip off the top sheet and use it for your purposes.

Most OpenDoc parts will be either distributed as stationery ready for embedding in documents or already incorporated into documents, possibly with links set up to other parts.

Summary

The basic OpenDoc concepts presented in this chapter differ from the concepts of many other computer environments in that they are very simple and remarkably non-computerese. If you were to try to explain the most basic aspects of OpenDoc to someone who is not well-versed in computers, they would likely look at you strangely—not because they wouldn't understand, but because you would be telling them something very obvious.

In approaching OpenDoc, many people with long experience with computers have problems with the concepts. They are impatient to know how it happens, and they try to correlate the OpenDoc world with the world they've come to know. They should resist the temptation to map OpenDoc concepts onto the world of monolithic applications, at least for the next few chapters. There, you will see how OpenDoc actually functions from the point of view of the user, the industry, and the computer software itself.

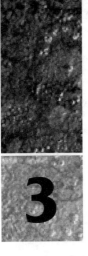

3

What Is OpenDoc?
The User's Answer

The basic components of OpenDoc—compound documents, containers, and parts—were described in Chapter 2, "Basic OpenDoc Concepts." They represent an evolution in the design of computer software. Yet in and of themselves, they are scarcely the revolution that OpenDoc as a whole promises to be. In this chapter, you will see how these simple concepts are combined into the new way of using computers that OpenDoc embodies.

This chapter focuses on the user's experience with OpenDoc: what OpenDoc looks like, how it feels to use OpenDoc software, and how OpenDoc differs from traditional software. In Chapter 4, OpenDoc will be examined from a different perspective, that of the developers and marketers of software who are interested in how OpenDoc will affect the industry.

The five main sections of this chapter deal with the user's experience with OpenDoc. In the first three, the new approach is explained as the importance of tasks, documents and components are discussed. While the transition to OpenDoc is significant, it is not cataclysmic, and the fourth section addresses transition issues. In the fifth, you will see what you can throw out and ignore from the "old" environment and what additional new issues you will need to deal with.

Using OpenDoc: Focusing on Tasks

With the exception of the parents, spouses, and close friends of programmers, most people are not interested in running programs or using operating systems. They want to write letters, balance their checkbooks, log on to on-line services, browse video, play games—generally, do things that make sense to them. A tremendous barrier has been erected between people and the tasks they want to do with their computers. This barrier consists of application programs, operating systems, and a vast assortment of mumbo-jumbo. Initially, people had no choice but to accept this as the cost of using a computer—a cost that (one hoped) would be offset by the improved efficiency the computer would provide once these barriers were overcome.

Clearing them away has proven difficult. New computer chips provide more and more processing power at lower and lower costs, but all too often this power is being harnessed to provide still more features and functionality in applications and operating systems. These added features make the software more complex than ever. However, some of this new processing power has been carefully squirreled away by developers who have attempted to reduce the difficulty of using computers by automating and simplifying steps that users must go through in order to begin doing the work they want to do. Sophisticated and processor-intensive technologies like speech synthesis, handwriting recognition, and active assistance are gaining more widespread use as a means of bringing the functionality of applications directly to users.

Still, the user is confronted with the need to learn how to use an application—a tool—in order to carry out a task. The complexity and steep learning curves of applications are simply frustrating barriers to the real work. While some past attempts have been made at focusing attention on the task rather than the tool, OpenDoc takes a significant and substantial step further. In a very real sense, there are no OpenDoc application programs; there are only your tasks and your data. You can't run an OpenDoc word processor or an OpenDoc spreadsheet. They don't exist.

What does exist is a document that contains data—your data.

Using OpenDoc: Focusing on Documents

Computers, from their beginnings, have had two roles: They are computational engines (the first ones having been designed to compute logarithms and other arithmetic tables), and they are data storage machines. In real life anecdote as well as popular mythology, stories about the difficulty of finding and manipulating data inside a computer have been told and retold, thereby becoming an accepted part of computer lore.

For both of the computer's traditional roles, data is required. Data has been considered as the raw material that is processed by computers. Everyone knows that vast amounts of data need to be fed in to the ever-hungry processor and that equally vast amounts need to be churned out on paper and storage media. In many computing environments, the raw material—data—is taken for granted and not treated with particularly high regard. The data management staffs of most organizations are not nearly so esteemed as their more "glamorous" colleagues on application development teams. Where data management is taught as part of computer science curricula, it is often an add-on, an elective that competes with a core curriculum devoted to designing, writing, and running programs.

All of this is somewhat mysterious because the user really cares *only* about data. The newspaper editor doesn't really care how a story's headline is typeset so long as it is clear, accurate, and attention-getting. The economist will gladly talk for hours about the meaning of half a dozen statistics, but (usually) will have no interest whatsoever in the program that computed and printed them out. By basically eliminating application programs from the environment, OpenDoc puts the focus back on data and the user.

The Old Way: Application-Centered Architecture

In traditional computing environments, you go through several steps before you can do productive work.

1. You decide what application program you need to use to do the task at hand (e.g., word processor, spreadsheet, page layout).

2. You start the application program.

3. You create a document.

4. You start to work by putting your data into the document.

There may be additional steps along the way. If the program does not handle all the tasks you need to do, you may have to stop in mid-stream and do the following steps.

5. You decide which additional program you need in order to do the specific task that you now need to do.

6. You start that program.

7. You either open the document you created before in this new program and manipulate it as you see fit, or you create a new document in the new program and import the data from the first program's document into it.

These processes may be repeated several times as you work on your task. As anyone who has been through this experience knows, the incorrect choice of an application program in steps 1 or 5 can be disastrous. Because not all applications can share data with others, it is remarkably easy to paint yourself into a corner. For example, most page layout programs allow you to import text and graphics from other applications. Most, however, do not allow you to export work done within them to other applications. Should you need to do so, you may have to back up several steps and repeat the work that you've done using another program that does allow the work to be exported.

One way of solving this problem has been for vendors to supply suites of applications that are guaranteed to work together. Unfortunately, this approach has several drawbacks:

1. It favors large, mass-market development efforts over those of smaller, often more innovative software developers.

2. Because no such application environment can ever be all-encompassing, it merely postpones the moment of reckoning. Sooner or later, users will want a feature or function that that integrated environment does not provide and will need to go through the data sharing/conversion process outlined previously.

3. The resulting integrated environments are bigger and more complex than are their component applications, thereby increasing the number and size of barriers to effective use.

This way of working on computers—an application-centered model—has been standard for nearly half a century. It worked very well in the mainframe environments, where staffs of specialists were available to actually run programs for users. These staffs were expert not only at running programs but also at converting data from one program's format to another's. This way of working is less successful in the personal computer environment, although it was satisfactory for the early adopters of this technology, since most of them either were familiar with mainframe environments and the ways in which programs were run or were willing to learn these techniques.

The need for specialists to actually run programs and to prepare data for them is little tolerated by personal computer users. Someone who has purchased a complete computer package for under $2,000 at the local appliance store is unlikely to look happily on the prospect of hiring a consultant to run it. People increasingly expect to be able to use their computers on their own and without help. Whereas the first computers were distinctive machines surrounded by specialized staffs and support equipment, today's personal computer is more likely to be perceived by its owner as something like a toaster or a radio: something that can be used without intermediaries by someone who wants to toast an English muffin or hear a few snatches of song.

The New Way: Document-Centered Architecture

As long as the application-centered model of computing is used, people will need to understand and know how to run applications—tasks that are by definition of secondary importance to them. Expertise in software is not on everyone's list of skills, so consultants will still need to be hired, courses attended, and endless calls to technical support hotlines made.

In a model of computing that is centered on tasks and data, it is reasonable to expect that people need to know and understand what they want to do and the information they need to manipulate. If they do not, it is equally reasonable to expect them to learn about these things. For example, if you want to balance your books, taking a course in bookkeeping is a relevant thing to do. Taking a course in how to run a bookkeeping application, however, would be a detour from your task.

Thus the focus on data and documents is a reasonable, natural focus for people who want to do work. A focus on application programs is a remnant of an older era of computing and a distraction for most people.

Where Are the Applications?

The functionality that applications provide can't go away, since it is needed to do the work. Although applications are fairly well hidden in the OpenDoc world, the diligent user can find files that provide functionality to the documents. These files differ from those of traditional applications in a number of ways. Most particularly, they cannot be run by themselves; they are invoked only when their documents are opened.

Many of the services that were provided by applications in the application-centered model are provided by OpenDoc itself; other services are provided by the documents that contain OpenDoc parts and by the parts themselves. This redistribution of functionality helps in the accomplishment of one of the major objectives of OpenDoc: being able to easily share data among several documents, and easily combine documents and parts of documents. OpenDoc consists of many subsystems, each with its own environment and each of which conforms to the OpenDoc standards so that they can all work together. (The next section describes OpenDoc's component structure in more depth.) One function that is inextricably linked to documents is data storage. In its implementation, OpenDoc addresses some of the fundamental difficulties that have arisen over the years with data management.

Data Management

Computers ultimately store information in a digitized form on electromagnetic media (hard disks, diskettes, magnetic tape), paper tape, optical media (CD-ROM discs), and other devices. In the traditional application-centered world, the formats of this information—both the codes for numbers and letters as well as the higher-level data layouts of records and files—vary from machine to machine and application program to application program. It is the rare computer user who has not confronted a diskette containing a document that simply cannot be read by the available software. Each application determines its own preferred file formats and uses them for its documents. (Some applications are good colleagues to others, that is they read and write files in a variety of formats that allow interchange with other applications.)

The difficulty of moving data among applications stems not only from each application's having developed its own data storage system and file layouts. It also results from the marketing strategy adopted by many companies that involves their maintaining a unique form of data storage in order to keep customers loyal to their products. For example, converting your personal financial data from one program's format to another may involve enough re-entry that you will think twice about switching to another vendor's software. As with the infamous "key diskettes" that were prevalent in the late 1980's when vendors implemented copy protection on their software, this strategy is anti-user. It protects the vendor at the cost of making life more difficult for users. There has been less outcry over the issue of incompatible and proprietary data formats than there was over the issue of copy protection. But this is only because the problem of incompatible data storage has existed since the beginning of the Computer Age. Unless a user accepts the proposition that all data will be stored in one application (or in one vendor's suite of applications), a certain amount of effort is always required to move data from one application to another. This effort—necessitated by incompatible data formats—is an unnecessary, unproductive task from the user's point of view. (After all, the data belongs to the user.)

OpenDoc provides a storage system that is based on each platform's native file-storage facilities and that is available to all OpenDoc components. Its developers use this standardized storage system, reading and writing their data in whatever formats are appropriate. This, together with OpenDoc's system-wide support for moving data among documents, makes the difficulties of incompatible formats far less a barrier to the completion of users' work than was the case in application-centered systems. To fully understand how this works, it is important to examine the documents and parts of documents that you work directly with and assemble as you carry out your work in an OpenDoc world.

Using OpenDoc: Focusing on Components

OpenDoc starts with the user, the task objective, and the data needed to complete the task. All three may be very complex (certainly the user is the most complex of all!), and different tools and ways of working are necessary as the work proceeds. Rather than fitting users, objectives, and data into a large predefined monolithic model called "Word Processing," OpenDoc lets you work with subtasks and portions of your data using the appropriate tools. As a project progresses, you add data, perform new subtasks, and incidentally incorporate new tools to the world of the OpenDoc document in which you are working.

OpenDoc assumes you will be combining parts of documents in new and different ways. This assumption also presupposes you will not first assemble all the tools you will ever need to carry out your task (as you do when you buy an enormous shrink-wrapped application). Rather, you will add and subtract tools as the work progresses. This is a reasonable assumption, since it is based on how people actually do complex tasks. The road from start to finish is never smooth; there are detours, leaps ahead, and occasional fallings-behind. One of the great virtues of Open-Doc is its assumption that people will actually work the way in which they have worked for thousands of years. One of the great failings of the application-centered model is its assumption that people will change their eons-old way of working in order to accommodate a machine.

Implications of Components: System Structure

For OpenDoc to work, its documents and their components must be easily combined and able to communicate with one another in a straightforward manner. The combinations and communications are not at the mercy of an all-powerful application, but are facilitated by OpenDoc's design. Each OpenDoc part is responsible for managing itself and supporting combination, communication, and integrated storage.

In the past, some applications have provided a certain degree of extensibility with add-ons and extensions. PhotoShop plug-ins, HyperCard XCMDs, and QuarkXPress Xtensions are all examples of technologies that allow third parties and end-users to augment the out-of-the-box application. Yet, these applications remain application-centered, and the add-ons and extensions are always called from the main program and are under its control.

OpenDoc assumes there is a degree of independence and equality among the components of a document. Even though the root part itself has certain larger responsibilities than some of its embedded parts, OpenDoc provides a structure in which the parts negotiate over issues that concern them, such as the area to use on the screen and the handling of user events. These negotiations are clearly specified in the documentation, even to the extent of providing the circumstances under which a specific part can "veto" another part's requests. There is no assumption that any one part of the system is more powerful than any other. The notion that OpenDoc parts will always be used and combined by users is central to the system. OpenDoc and its parts do not presuppose what the users' results will be.

Implications of Components: Where They Come From

A consequence of OpenDoc's component-based structure, in which all components can easily interact with others, is that people can assemble various groups of components to accomplish their objectives. Because OpenDoc clearly defines the interfaces and interoperability standards, components from different vendors can work together as easily (sometimes more so) than different application programs from a single vendor have done in the past.

This, of course, is one of the great benefits to the user of OpenDoc. For example, suppose Word Processor A has a grammar-checking tool that you particularly like, but Word Processor B manages columnar text much better than Word Processor A does. In the application-centered environment, you have to choose one program over the other. With OpenDoc, you can assemble the particular components desired into a document that reflects your work and the way you want to do it.

As you will see in Chapter 4, "What Is OpenDoc? The Business Answer," this has the potential to change the way in which software is distributed. Some people will happily jump into the world of components, mixing and matching them in various ways until they come up with precisely what they want. This is a natural human activity, shown repeatedly in the lives of people who get satisfaction from redecorating their homes and offices or from assembling elaborate component-based entertainment systems. For other people, it is much easier and more satisfying to hire a decorator to mix and match upholstery and curtains or to buy an "all-in-one" TV/stereo/VCR that you simply plug into the wall outlet.

The fact that a user can combine components from many sources into your documents doesn't necessarily mean that *you* will do it. If you want to, you will be able to, and later chapters of this book will provide you with guidelines for finding and evaluating components. If you prefer the "hire a decorator" approach, system integrators and consultants can provide combinations of components targeted to individuals and specific markets. You will even find shrink-wrapped boxes in your local computer store that on the outside will look like those big monolithic applications of yore but on the inside will be a combination of OpenDoc components targeted to individual markets and uses.

Thus the monolithic applications of the past are gone, replaced by parts and part editors, containers, and documents. While this provides an improved user experience (chiefly by providing more control and power to the user), it is nonetheless a disconcerting move for many people.

Concerns about Components

Having mainframe computers was very reassuring in some ways. Granted, they were very expensive to buy and maintain, they required specialized support staffs (everyone from air-conditioning specialists to data librarians), and they were extraordinarily vulnerable to disruptions of communications and power utilities. Still, a mainframe represented the core of an organization: You could look at it and know that inside its walls all of the corporate data was (somehow) stored. You could see the cables and telephone wires that connected scores or hundreds of terminals to it. In most companies that used mainframe computers, the mainframe was included on tours that proud CEO's gave to their colleagues and customers.

In many companies, mainframe computers have been replaced by networks of personal computers. There is no computer room to show off. The hub is gone. While a decentralized structure for a computing environment is demonstrably more stable than a centralized one, you can't go look at some machine that is the nerve center of the organization.

To a certain extent, OpenDoc implements a similar change within the desktop computer. The big applications, like the big mainframes, are gone. They take with them all of their complexities but leave in their wake a multitude of small pieces distributed all over the place, as well as a lingering feeling of uncertainty about just exactly where everything has gone to.

It is not sufficient just to say that OpenDoc will manage everything. The disquiet and uncertainty are real. OpenDoc design addressed these issues from the beginning, both in the practical and the psychological aspects. OpenDoc employs several stratagems to address these issues:

- By formalizing the interfaces of parts, their data storage, and their communications, OpenDoc protects itself and its parts from failures that could ripple through the system.

- It has been assumed that parts and documents may find themselves in environments that are not explicitly prepared for them. Parts are designed to be opened in a number of different ways. A missing code library should not result in a disabled OpenDoc document.

- CI Labs has been formed to certify the part editors that comply with the OpenDoc standards. Their testing designs and facilities, which are available to developers who request formal certification as well as to others, are designed to address the issues of interoperability and robustness.

What It Looks Like: Parts and Their Palettes

What, then, does OpenDoc look like? Open a new document in any drawing program you have. Now double-click on the Draw part in the OpenDoc examples on the OpenDoc CD-ROM. Can you spot the differences? Any difference? There are few or none. While OpenDoc represents a dramatic change in the way in which software is written, from the user's point of view it need not appear in any way different from traditional applications. Compare the Draw part's palette with that of your traditional drawing application.

The palettes and toolbars provide similar functionality and have comparable designs. They differ in how they behave. In the traditional application, the application itself is responsible for maintaining the palettes. Their contents may change as the user clicks on different parts of the document (text, graphics, and so on). From the application's menus, the user can select which palettes are shown or hidden; with the mouse, the user can move the application palettes around. When the palettes change, they do so within the context *and shape* of the application's palette windows and toolbars.

With OpenDoc, the palettes are managed by each part of the document. Thus they come and go as you click on different parts of the document. They need not fit into the application's predefined palette shape, but use the size and shape that they need. Each OpenDoc part has its own environment of menus, palettes, and commands that are available when the part is active. These parts and their environments function in the same way no matter where they are.

At first glance, this coming and going of palettes might appear confusing or disturbing to the user. In fact, it is not and is quite natural. People are quite capable of keeping track of a number of different frames of reference and work environments without confusing them. For example, imagine yourself at your desk at home catching up on paying your monthly bills. You may have your bank statement, your checkbook, a roll of stamps, and a pile of bills all arranged on your desk. As you work, you reach for these things, and after a few moments, you do not even need to look to know exactly where, say, the stamps are, since you have a kinesthetic memory of the activity of reaching for them.

Next, say, the phone rings. A friend is calling to suggest you take in a movie together. Your frame of reference has moved physically to the telephone and mentally to your friend and your excursion to the movies. After a brief conversation, you reach for the newspaper, and—with new physical and mental frames of reference— find the schedule of the movie that you have decided on.

After you hang up and return to your bills, you will most likely be able to reach for your stamps again without looking for them. Within the context of this bill-paying activity, the tools that you have arranged are familiar and in their "natural" places.

Someone observing you may see a great deal of activity as you manipulate envelopes, checkbook, telephone, and newspaper. From your point of view, however, you are doing only three simple things: paying your bills, answering the phone, and arranging to go the movies. Part of the power of OpenDoc is that it fits in so naturally with the way in which people actually do work.

Still, there are cases where a uniform "look" is desired or where a constant set of tools should be available to the user no matter what part of the OpenDoc document is active. OpenDoc, ever flexible, allows an alternative interface to accommodate this need.

What It Looks Like: Suite Extensions

OpenDoc parts can be written in such a way that they do not directly provide a user interface of menus and palettes; they may rely on another part of the document to provide this functionality. In this scenario, a special part—whose function is only to manage interface issues—is added to the document and serves as liaison between the user and the actual parts that contain data and do the work. Because all OpenDoc parts respond to commands sent from other parts, it is of no concern to a part whether it responds directly to a user's mouse click or to a command sent from another part that has actually received the mouse click.

The implication of this concept is one of the more exciting aspects of OpenDoc. If a part can use another part (or several parts) to construct its interface, that interface can itself be moved in and out of the document. Not only can you mix and match the functionality that you want, but you can choose the interface that drives it all. From a certain viewpoint, the interface is just another functionality of the entire activity a user undertakes. Is it really any more different to replace one spell-checker with another than it is to replace one interface with another? Once again, OpenDoc provides a path that can lead to highly customized and useful software.

The possibility of changing interfaces is very intriguing. You can think of internationalization—changing the language of the interface. Then again, you might think of changing the complexity of the interface—from novice to pro. Or, the interface change might reflect the age of the user. Perhaps a new rite of passage will emerge, alongside such traditional ones as the removal of bicycle training wheels and the acquisition of a driving license. What better gift for the elementary school graduate than a grown-up interface to the family's Internet navigator!

Extensions may be added to OpenDoc by parts to allow them to communicate among themselves. In providing a transportable interface, the parts that provide the functionality may share a specific extension that facilitates their actions; an interface part that is visible to the user can provide the feedback and control to the user while communicating directly with the extension and indirectly with the other parts.

Changing interfaces in this way is quite simple and straight-forward—provided that the underlying parts are all there. Obviously it can't be done with traditional applications; hybrid applications that are in transition from traditional architectures to OpenDoc will find it hard to support such a feature. Furthermore, this paradigm will often rely on "faceless" parts that depend on other parts and extensions to reveal their functionality. For these reasons, changeable interfaces may well be part of the second generation of OpenDoc. On the other hand, the prospect is so intriguing to developers and users (and so potentially profitable) that this functionality may appear sooner rather than later.

"Faceless" parts, which depend on other parts and extensions to reveal their functionality, may well be part viewers—which developers are likely to freely distribute. If someone wants to manipulate the part and its data, they will simply buy the interface. In most discussions of OpenDoc, the assumption has been that what will be bought will be a part editor. However, nothing prevents the developer from implementing a design where the functionality is unlocked with an interface part. That architectural design and its implementation really shouldn't concern a user. Users who want to manipulate parts and their data just want to buy an interface. It's up to developers to provide it—and OpenDoc has an intriguing array of choices that can be used.

Using OpenDoc: Making the Transition

While OpenDoc represents a major change in the way in which software is developed and distributed, it can represent no change—or a significant change—in the way in which people actually use software. The ability of users to make a smooth transition to OpenDoc, and even to reverse the process and use OpenDoc with traditional applications that may survive on personal computers or mainframes, is a critical part of OpenDoc's strategy.

It need not be an either/or process. In this book, you will see how to develop and use solutions that are based solely on OpenDoc and its features as well as how to integrate OpenDoc into existing ("legacy") systems.

Using OpenDoc: Getting Rid of Old Baggage

One of the biggest mistakes you can make in learning about OpenDoc is to try to map it to your concepts of computer applications as they existed in the past. OpenDoc is a simpler and more structured way of working with computers. Just as you would when trying to learn a foreign language, look at OpenDoc on its own without trying to translate its concepts back into the terminology of an outmoded technology.

Summary

In this chapter, you saw the user's perspective of OpenDoc: Its focus on you and your tasks, on the data and documents you create and manipulate, and on the components that are assembled to help you accomplish these goals. OpenDoc represents a new way of working in the computer world, albeit one that has been a natural way of working for humans for thousands of years.

The shift away from monolithic mass-market applications and toward a component-based architecture is significant for the entire software industry. The next chapter examines those issues.

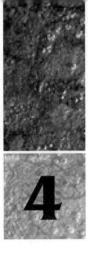

4

What Is OpenDoc?
The Business Answer

In Chapter 3, you saw the implications of OpenDoc for individual computer users, the primary one being that it helps individuals focus on their tasks. Now it is time to look at what OpenDoc means from a business perspective for three groups: software developers, enterprise developers, and systems integrators. Some of the implications for these groups are shared and some are different.

OpenDoc is an open, platform-neutral standard; as such it differs markedly from most of the software that is on the market today. This open standard is maintained by Component Integration Laboratories (CI Labs), the nonprofit organization that supports OpenDoc. OpenDoc has implications for software publishers and developers, those people who create shrink-wrapped software sold in stores. OpenDoc may well bring changes to economic models for the software industry. In-house developers (who create software that is typically used only within their own organizations), systems integrators, and value-added resellers (VARs, companies who try to solve business problems by combining technologies with their customers' existing systems) will also see their businesses changed by OpenDoc.

OpenDoc Is an Open Standard

OpenDoc is supported by an alliance of companies committed to an open adoption process that does not unduly favor a single vendor or architecture. The alliance—started by Apple Computer, IBM, and Novell/WordPerfect—then formed a nonprofit organization, Component Integration Laboratories. Since then, quite a few other companies have joined, including both large and small software companies.

CI Labs is a clearinghouse for the technologies that are part of OpenDoc; it licenses those technologies to the members of CI Labs. However CI Labs is run differently than other industry consortia, such as the Object Management Group, in that it accepts only technologies that have at least one existing implementation. This is because when a consortium is considering a new technology that exists solely on paper, people have an understandable but sometimes unfortunate tendency to argue for a solution regardless of its practicality or ramifications. They do this for both idealistic reasons and pragmatic, commercial reasons. However, if a consortium were to adopt a company's unimplemented proposal with no changes, doing so might give that company an edge over the other consortium members. This kind of politics ultimately has the effect of delaying implementations of the standard under discussion. By accepting only working implementations, CI Labs has successfully avoided these kinds of political issues.

OpenDoc Software Will Be Certified

CI Labs also realized the importance of certifying implementations of OpenDoc components. It maintains certification processes for its members who are porting OpenDoc services to new platforms. Also, it supports a certification service for vendors to ensure their part editors follow the standards. It further provides a test suite that will enable an OpenDoc developer to self-certify that its Open-Doc parts comply with the OpenDoc standards. This is a lower level of certification, but it is also less expensive, thereby enabling smaller developers to still participate in the certification process. Consumers of OpenDoc parts are well advised to purchase certified parts, since far fewer problems should occur with them.

Contacting CI Labs

Other activities that CI Labs supports are the promotion of standard formats for exporting data and the coordination of

OpenDoc extensions. Membership in CI Labs is open to anyone, including platform vendors, software developers, and software users. For information about membership in CI Labs, contact them as follows:

Component Integration Laboratories
P.O. Box 61747
Sunnyvale, CA 94088-1747

Telephone: 408/864-0300
Fax: 408/864-0380
Internet: cilabs@cilabs.org

OpenDoc for Software Developers

OpenDoc changes many aspects of the software business as it affects developers. Small developers may find themselves playing a larger role in the OpenDoc world, while for all developers, OpenDoc's extensibility, cross-platform support, and scriptability will change how they work.

The Rise of Suites and the Decline of the Small Developer's Role

Small developers have not played a significant role in the software industry in the last decade. Even a successful "small" developer today, such as Netscape, has resources far greater than those of a "small" developer in the past. This is partly because the cost of marketing, selling, and supporting a product can easily exceed the cost of developing it. Perhaps the more important factor is that intellectual capital within current products, such as Adobe PageMaker or Novell WordPerfect, is almost inconceivably more complex than that in equivalent products of 10 years ago, such as WordStar. The amount of functionality in current products is overwhelming—the checklist of features is enormous compared with products from a decade ago. Today, however, the software is only a part of the product. Also often included are extensive documentation, training materials (perhaps including video tapes), on-line help, and examples. If the present situation continues, smaller developers will have no hope except to pick niche markets that are of no interest (they hope) to the larger developers. In short, the barrier to market entry is no longer technology.

Over the last five years, this situation has worsened as the software industry has moved towards suites and away from individual applications. The release and widespread marketing of Microsoft Office greatly accelerated this trend. This has had a major impact on the software industry, tending to further reduce the potential impact of smaller developers. The rapid evolution of suites has raised the financial, developmental, and organizational barriers to becoming a successful software publisher. Even other large software vendors, such as Novell (actually its Word-Perfect division) and Lotus (now part of IBM) have difficulty competing with Microsoft Office.

OpenDoc Provides a Role for Small Developers

Software will continue to be sold in suites, but as more developers adopt OpenDoc, some of these will evolve into suites of OpenDoc parts rather than large, relatively unwieldy parts. Small developers, however, will potentially play a role, since it will be much easier to integrate third-party parts into an OpenDoc-based suite than into large monolithic applications. OpenDoc provides the first significant business opportunity for small developers in a decade.

Large Monolithic Applications Are a Problem

There are also some strong technical reasons why developers should adopt OpenDoc. A significant side effect of software's commercial success has been the large increase in application size. Only 10 years ago, you could expect to have your operating system and at least one application on a floppy disk and still be able to work off the floppy disk. Today some applications are shipped on CD-ROMs because the applications are so large and there are so many auxiliary files (e.g., help and examples) that come along with the product. Today, an application that requires 5MB of disk space is considered small.

Another noticeable difference between the software industry of today and that of a decade ago is the long time it takes to create and release new versions of software. And, no matter what schedule developers give, they always seem to be delivering late. Examples of this are operating systems such as Windows 95 (delivered three years late) and Apple's System 7. Other examples are application software such as new versions of Adobe Page-Maker and Microsoft Word. Why is this happening?

Object-Oriented Programming Languages Are Not Enough

The vast majority of successful applications and operating systems were developed using procedural languages such as C or Pascal. The code bases and architectural designs of these products may be more than 10 years old, although probably none of the original code is still in use. Would the use of object-oriented languages, such as C++ help? Undoubtably it would, although it is quite difficult to retrofit an object-oriented architecture into an existing product, especially one with a large code base. However, this question avoids a larger and more important issue: whether one-size-fits-all-users software is still appropriate. A related question is whether some functions are integral to a piece of software; for example, should a word processor include functions for creating and editing tables, or should a spreadsheet include graphing and charting features. Many of today's software engineering problems are the result of success, that is, today's software has reached certain limits in the current technology.

OpenDoc Provides Much-Needed Concepts for Managing Complexity

There is no question that object-oriented programming languages, such as C++ and Smalltalk, have provided the next evolutionary step in software development. In particular, this is because an object-oriented language provides better technology for managing the complexities within an application. However, it does not solve the problem of developing and maintaining large monolithic applications. Large applications, even those developed using C++, are still difficult to test, document and support. The complexity that can be reduced with an object-oriented language tends to be implementational complexity, not the complexity of large architectures. This type of complexity can be resolved by the use of an architectural concept called component software. OpenDoc was designed from the start to be an architecture for component software. It not only provides part editors as a way of separating distinct sets of functions (such as separating charting from the calculation engine of a spreadsheet). It also provides several other mechanisms for architecting software, namely extensions, plug-ins and services. An extension is a programming interface for an OpenDoc part that enables a client to establish high bandwidth connections or tight integration with a part. An extension interface can either be private (proprietary) or public. A plug-in extends the capabilities of the OpenDoc shell or functionality to the current Open-Doc session. Services are special OpenDoc parts that implement specialized services of interest to other parts and documents, such as spell checking. Services tend to have less user interface and tend not to save information into documents. OpenDoc also naturally supports distributed computing, that is, parts can communicate with one another even if they are running on different computers.

The flexibility of OpenDoc parts, extensions, plug-ins, and services provide some architectural relief to developers whose only choice today is the monolithic application. OpenDoc provides a flexible, expandable environment that can support metaphors and realities as diverse as documents, networks, and databases.

OpenDoc provides several different ways of modularizing a set of functions, thereby giving developers more than one option. Software will be implemented as smaller pieces than it is today. This will tend to shorten development and testing cycles, as well as enable developers to react more quickly to the changing marketplace.

OpenDoc Provides Support for Multiple Platforms

While it is true that Microsoft Windows has captured the majority of desktop computers, the market has still endorsed a number of other desktop platforms, including the Mac OS and OS/2. Naturally, as the cost of developing and maintaining a large application has risen, the cost of doing so on two or three platforms has risen even more so. Software developers, squeezed from above by dropping prices and from below by increasing costs, must become more economical. The costs of cross-platform development have increased not only because of the expansion of required functionality, but also from the increasing depth and complexity of the operating systems on which applications live. Developing software on a cross-platform basis is therefore difficult for a variety of reasons.

OpenDoc does not eliminate all of these cross-platform difficulties, but it does make significant progress towards easing them. From the start, OpenDoc was conceived as a cross-platform architecture, providing platform-neutral APIs and interface guidelines. Among the platform-neutral software packages that comprise OpenDoc are the OpenDoc class library, Bento persistent-object storage services, Open Scripting Architecture, System Object Model, and ComponentGlue. OpenDoc, on the other hand, does not provide platform-independent imaging or graphics services, so there are still some difficult technical problems that remain to be solved.

OpenDoc will be supported on six platforms: Windows 95, Windows 3.1, the Mac OS, OS/2, AIX, and UNIX (Motif). Various OpenDoc-aware development tools support cross-platform development, including Apple's ODF C++ framework, Novell's AppWare visual development environment, and Oracle's Power Objects.

OpenDoc Can Be Easily Extended to Support New Data Types

The last decade has brought many new data types for developers to create, manipulate, and store. Twenty years ago, the only common data types were simple (single-font) text and various types of numbers. With the release of the Apple Macintosh in the mid-1980s, some new data types became available, such as complex styled text with multiple fonts and writing systems, black-and-white bitmapped graphics, simple object-oriented graphics, and basic sounds. Five years ago, color graphics and more-complex kinds of sound (such as MIDI) were added to the mix. More recently, developers and users have become habituated to digital video playback (basic multimedia) and hypertext. Today there is a great deal of excitement about URLs, courtesy of the World Wide Web, and two-way video (video conferencing). Not all of these data types and media are appropriate for all applications, but most applications could minimally support most of them in some fashion. This profusion of data types adds to the complexity of monolithic applications.

OpenDoc makes it easy to extend support to new media types, since it was designed as a compound-document architecture. OpenDoc parts, if they support embedding at all, will support the embedding of new parts containing new data types by design. OpenDoc therefore makes it easy for applications to support new data types.

OpenDoc Provides Strong Support for Extensibility and Scriptability

As users grow in their understanding and knowledge of software, they want their software to adapt to their way of working rather than the other way around. Users can mold software to suit their particular requirements provided the software includes suitable means for doing so. Scriptability, the capability of acting on high-level commands coming from a client, enables the user to integrate software components into a system and to automate repetitive tasks. Extensibility provides a method for developers to extend an application by creating external (to the software) code segments that the user can execute from the application.

OpenDoc promotes scriptability by providing the Open Scripting Architecture (OSA) as a basic part of OpenDoc services. OSA is not a scripting language, but rather a framework that supports scripting languages. OpenDoc supports extensibility by providing several mechanisms that developers can choose to adopt, including parts, extensions, plug-ins, and services.

A New Economic Model for Software?

There are several ways in which OpenDoc might change current economic models for the packaged software business or even bring about new ones. Developers need to understand how their business might be affected by the success of OpenDoc. It is clear that smaller developers have a shrinking role in today's software business, even more so as the wave of mergers and acquisitions runs through the industry. OpenDoc may well change that—with implications for both large and small developers.

Small developers have played a very important role in the software industry. Many innovative products have come from them, rather than from large developers. Examples include Microsoft PowerPoint (which was originally developed by Forethought), Aldus PageMaker (Aldus was originally a small developer), AutoDesk AutoCAD, Mosaic (the first WWW browser), Netscape, and ClarisWorks. If in the future small developers have a smaller place in this industry, then the pace of innovation will slow.

How might OpenDoc affect the economics of software publishing? There are three possibilities:

1. Replacement of large applications by suites of part editors
2. Moving large applications into large part editors
3. Marketing of a variety of small parts

Gradual Evolution: Dinosaurs Die Off; Mammals Take Over

The first possibility is that monolithic applications will eventually be replaced by suites of OpenDoc part editors. Instead of selling a monolithic application in a shrink-wrapped box, a publisher will sell the suite of OpenDoc part editors in that same shrink-wrapped box. Users of such products may not notice that they are using OpenDoc-based software. The publisher will see benefits from this evolution in the form of fewer problems in meeting product schedules, reduced time to test the product, reduced time to document the product, and smaller support costs. This incremental adoption of OpenDoc may make the most sense for larger publishers, which will have the most difficult time moving to a component architecture.

The Big Part Theory

A similar, second possibility is that some publishers will migrate monolithic applications into monolithic part editors. If this happens, then the publisher will see less of the benefits than if it were to migrate into smaller, more coherent part editors. This is because the software base for their OpenDoc parts will still be too large in the sense that it will contain more than one set of related functions and the development processes will remain similar to what they were before the migration to OpenDoc. Users will receive smaller benefits because such OpenDoc parts will take longer to open than will other parts and because the interface will tend to be more complex than might be otherwise possible.

There will definitely be some OpenDoc container applications that are similar to large OpenDoc parts. This will happen because it takes some time to migrate a large code base to a new architecture such as OpenDoc. Publishers will have to amortize development costs over time, and moving first to a container rather than directly to part editors will make financial sense. One can hope that this will be a short-term phenomenon as publishers move products over to OpenDoc part editors. Apple is providing a code library known as CALib (for Container Application Library) to make this a relatively painless process.

The Small Part Theory

In the third possibility, if OpenDoc is really successful, then there will be many new parts that will provide specific, coherent functionality. This will mean there will be market demand for a wide assortment of different parts that the large developers will not be able to satisfy by themselves. Smaller developers will have an important role in satisfying the demands of both primary and secondary (niche) markets. Certainly systems integrators and VARs will benefit from this. In fact, they may be some of the biggest winners.

Changes in Sales Channels

How OpenDoc will affect the current sales channels for software distribution and sales is not clear. For the larger publishers, the current situation can support the evolution of visible and well-marketed products to OpenDoc with few or no changes required.

The methods by which smaller software components can be sold will have to evolve from today's channels. The sudden and surprising success of Visual Basic components (VBXs) in the Windows market has shown that at least developers can quickly adapt to component software. The more difficult question is how quickly the user will adapt.

One factor that may play an important role in the establishment, growth, and success of a user marketplace for component software is the recent explosion of interest in on-line services, especially the exponential growth of the World Wide Web on the Internet. As this book is being written, standards for on-line commerce have just been agreed upon by the vast majority of players in the world of on-line services. Thus, as OpenDoc enters the market, a means of purchasing and installing software components is simultaneously becoming available. On-line services may be the catalyst for the rapid growth of the component software business.

OpenDoc for Developers in the Enterprise Realm

Finally, take a look at how OpenDoc affects developers who work in the enterprise realm. There are two groups of such developers: (1) in-house developers, who create software for use within their organizations, and (2) systems integrators and VARs, who create software for use by organizations within a particular vertical market or functional area. (Examples of vertical markets are banking, insurance, manufacturing, and biotechnology. Examples of functional areas are sales force automation, finance, and human relations.)

The enterprise realm includes both large- and medium-sized businesses. (Many small business environments are more similar to the home office than to a large business, hence the recent development of the acronym SOHO, for Small Office/Home Office.) It also includes the public sector, which in the U.S. consists of the federal, state, and local government organizations, as well as segments of the K–12 and higher-education markets.

Only minor differences exist in how OpenDoc will affect in-house developers versus VARs. In this section, the term *in-house developer* includes developers who work for systems integrators and VARs.

Computers in the enterprise realm function in a very different environment than do those used at home or in a small business, including the following:

1. The needs and requirements within the organization may be strong enough to support the development and maintenance of custom software.

2. These computers are usually connected to other computers through local area networks (LAN) and/or wide area networks (WAN). Standalone computers are relatively uncommon. Support for communications, networking, and distributed computing is essential.

3. The selection of both hardware and software is often controlled by organizational policies rather than by the individual user. In many organizations, multiple desktop platforms are often purchased by different internal groups, thereby creating pressure for support of cross-platform development.

Satisfying the Demand for Custom Software

Information Systems (IS) departments have been creating custom software since they came into existence. But only recently have most IS departments developed systems that utilize desktop computers. In the last several years, client-server architecture has enabled some organizations to take better advantage of their desktop computers. There are probably few companies today who don't have more computing power on their collective desktops than in their computer centers.

In-house applications are expensive to develop and maintain, as anyone who has ever done it can testify. Costs for a single system might range from a few thousand dollars on the low end (perhaps for a simple program written in Visual Basic) to many millions of dollars for complex systems. Unfortunately, at this time most IS budgets are decreasing, as are IS staff sizes. Pressure is on to develop more systems more rapidly with less money and fewer people.

Further, the demands of users with respect to in-house software are getting more difficult to satisfy. The increased quality of commercial software over the last decade has resulted in users' expecting in-house systems to be of the same quality. Users also expect regular updates and good documentation, as well as high-quality technical support. The cost of commercial software is often less than several hundred dollars per seat. Users generally don't understand why in-house systems are so costly and take so long to develop.

What are developers to do? Developing a large monolithic application is almost completely out of the question today, even if it was possible in the past. OpenDoc provides a better way of satisfying the demand for in-house applications, since it is now possible to create custom OpenDoc parts that can use commercial parts to provide some of the required functions. No longer will in-house developers have to implement common text or standard kinds of services such as text editing services or charting services, since these will be available as off-the-shelf parts. Instead, they will be able to focus on satisfying the requirements that are unique to their organization.

Satisfying the Requirements for Connectivity

Many organizations are moving away from host-based systems towards client/server architecture. The rapid growth of the Internet and the World Wide Web has captured the attention even of senior-level management, who typically are not technically oriented. Organizations are being forced to move towards on-line services as a means of distributing and disseminating information, both to internal and external audiences.

OpenDoc does not directly support networking, communications, or the connectivity to on-line services; however, it does provide an architecture that is compatible with them. Apple has created a product, named Cyberdog, which provided the first compelling example of how a complex application can be implemented on top of the OpenDoc architecture. Cyberdog provides access to a multitude of Internet-related services. (Cyberdog is discussed in Chapter 14.)

OpenDoc does provide support for distributed computing. One of the basic OpenDoc components is the System Object Model (SOM, discussed in Chapter 6). OpenDoc also supports the Distributed System Object Model (DSOM), a set of extensions to SOM that enables developers to create distributed applications.

Satisfying the Need for Cross-Platform Support

It is often hard to locate commercial software that runs on the multiple platforms used by an organization, once you get beyond the standard horizontal applications such as word processors and spreadsheets. This is especially true for vertical software applications.

OpenDoc and many of the OpenDoc-aware development tools support cross-platform development, thereby making it possible for organizations to support more than one desktop platform with a much smaller effect on their budget.

Summary

OpenDoc has the potential to radically alter the business of developing software. The balance between large and small developers may well change, the barrier to market entry, which has shifted from technology to other factors, may well change again.

These changes will affect all developers large and small, as well as enterprise developers of all sizes.

Part II

OpenDoc Technical
Overview

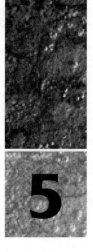

5

Overview of OpenDoc Technology

In the previous chapters, OpenDoc was examined from the outside—from the perspective of users and observers. In this chapter is an overview of the inside of OpenDoc—the technical issues and procedures that make it all possible.

The first section of this chapter is a walk-through of an OpenDoc solution involving three of the sample parts distributed with the OpenDoc SDK. The second section of this chapter provides an overview of the OpenDoc software itself—the software that runs when any OpenDoc document or part is active.

A Walk-through of an OpenDoc Solution

In Chapter 1, you saw how a simple word processing example became quite complex very quickly. Certainly the user interface shown in Figure 1-8 is quite daunting—it contains status information, tools for manipulating text, and tools for manipulating an image. Even the relatively simple operation shown in Figure 1-5 (copying and pasting styled text) poses serious interface and behavior issues, if you consider whether the user really wants to copy all of the styling information—including the foreign font—to the first document.

Traditional applications manage the interchange of data by being able to read and write a multitude of data types, either directly, through a translation mechanism, or indirectly, through common interchange formats. The complexity of the data (such as the underlining, italicizing, and font information shown in the example in Chapter 1) must be able to be written out by the sending application and read in by the receiving application (even if they are the same application). Each feature that is added to the application may require modifications to the data interchange structures.

OpenDoc, by comparison, is an environment in which parts assume from the beginning that they will embed within them parts about which they know little more than their identification and where in the container they are placed. Many of the examples of OpenDoc that were shown in its early days focused on the effects that can be achieved by embedding a multitude of different parts (text, graphics, video, real-time stock tickers, clocks that update themselves, and so on). The example chosen for this chapter is very simple and closely resembles the example used in Chapter 1. In this case, however, using OpenDoc, the result of copying and pasting styled text and images is not the rather peculiar and somewhat ghastly multitude of interfaces that accumulate into Figure 1-8.

A Simple Containing Part with an Embedded Part in It

Figure 5-1 shows an OpenDoc containing part with a part embedded in it. The container is shown in a window, which has a default name given by OpenDoc. When you open an OpenDoc part, by default it is named with the name of its part (in this case "container" was the name of the first OpenDoc part created). Affixed to the part name is the date and a unique serial number, if this is not the first such part created.

Note that creating a new OpenDoc container automatically creates a disk file. Some users may neglect to save their work as they go, but with OpenDoc it is impossible to create a new document and not have at least some record of it.

(A small cheer will go up from users who have worked literally for hours on a document that then disappeared into the ether of RAM. Until the user saves the OpenDoc document it may not contain data, but the document itself will exist.)

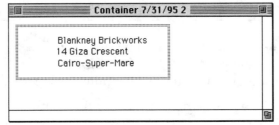

Figure 5-1.

An OpenDoc containing part with an embedded part

The embedded part contains three lines of text and is outlined in Figure 5-1 with a border indicating that it is active—its contents can be selected and modified.

Moving an Embedded Part from One Part to Another

In Figure 5-2, you see two OpenDoc containers. The one in the foreground is the same container with the same part in it that you saw in Figure 5-1. In the background, another part with a text part embedded in it is shown. By clicking on the embedded part, you can drag it from one containing part and drop it into another.

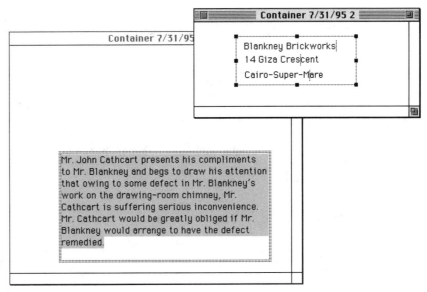

Figure 5-2.

Two OpenDoc containing parts

The result of this drag-and-drop procedure is shown in Figure 5-3: One container now contains two parts.

You can click on either part to activate it. If you click on the second line of text in the address part, the result will be as shown in Figure 5-4.

Embedded Parts May Themselves Contain Other Parts

The active border around the second line of text in the address part shows that it is an OpenDoc part and that it is active. The document in Figure 5-4 contains six OpenDoc parts:

1. The root part, which contains all other parts.
2. A text part containing the body of the letter ("Mr. John Cathcart presents..."). This is the Text Editor sample part from the OpenDoc SDK.
3. An embedded part that contains the address. This is the part shown outlined in Figure 5-3. (It is the Test Container part as distributed on the OpenDoc SDK.)
4. An embedded Text Editor part in the embedded Test Container part (#3), which contains the name ("Blankney Brickworks"). In this case it is a text part, but as you will see later, it could be any other type of part.

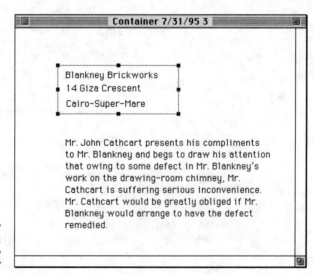

Figure 5-3.

Result of dragging a part from one part to another

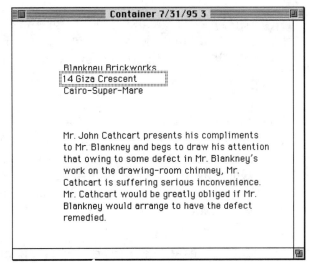

Figure 5-4.

Clicking on an embedded embedded part

5. Another embedded Text Editor part in the Test Container part. This one contains the second line of the address ("14 Giza Crescent"). It can be any type of part.

6. A third embedded part that contains the third line of the address ("Cairo-Super-Mare"). It is in the Test Container part.

Putting the Parts Together in a Different Way— A Mailing List

The parts shown in Figure 5-4 are quite simple. The use to which they are put is simpler still. The power of OpenDoc starts to become apparent as the parts are figuratively tossed in the air and rearranged as they come down into a related but very different solution.

The scenario given here is described from the point of view of a user. The same steps, however, could quite easily be played out in the offices of a software developer, a systems integrator, a solution provider, or a value-added reseller. All of these people periodically look at their products, tasks, and tools and ask how each could be made more powerful, more simple, or more productive. As anyone who has watched the "feature-creep" advance of monster applications knows, the desire to add more functionality to an application or process is not confined to users whose enthusiasm has gotten out of control.

One of the ODF sample parts is called ODFTable. It implements a very basic table/spreadsheet functionality. Each row and column of the table can be resized, and each cell can contain any other OpenDoc part. The dimensions of the cells on a page can be set and each can contain an OpenDoc part, so it is easy to drag the Test Container part containing the addresses into a cell of the table, as shown in Figure 5-5.

Although this example may seem overly simple and obvious, it is a fine example of the power of OpenDoc. You can very easily transform the ODFTable example program into a solution that is custom-designed to print mailing labels. If you add a menu containing popular mailing label dimensions, it is trivial to automatically adjust the cell sizes to match each dimension. An "Other…" menu item would allow the user to specify nonstandard sizes. (The only other significant feature required in a mailing label program is the ability to sort the labels. In Chapter 8, "Managing OpenDoc Communications: OSA," you'll see how to

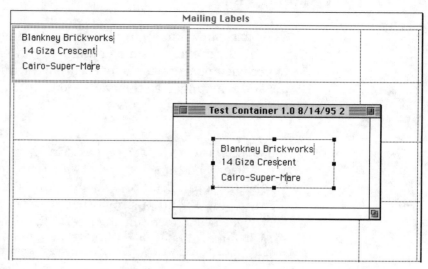

Figure 5-5.
ODFTable example becomes a mailing label solution

do that.) This little mailing list solution is complete and in fact can print mailing labels of more complexity than most products on the market today.

All the mailing list solution does is divide up each page into specially sized cells that may contain OpenDoc parts. If a cell has an OpenDoc part within it, the mailing list asks that part to draw or print itself in the appropriate location. The mailing list solution is so simple that it pays to examine a few points of interest, which is done in the following several sections.

Selection versus Activation

At this point, you may notice a difference in the highlighting of the embedded part shown in Figure 5-5 and the apparently similar part shown in Figure 5-1. OpenDoc's Human Interface Guidelines differentiate between active parts and selected parts. Only one part in a document can be active at a time. The active part is designated by the border shown in Figure 5-1 and in the background document in Figure 5-5. The Part Editor for a document's active part typically—though not always—controls the menus for that document; input from the mouse or keyboard normally flows to the active part. In technical terms, it has acquired the *selection focus*.

Embedded parts can normally be resized within their containing parts. To resize anything, you must first select it. The highlighting shown in Figure 5-5 shows that the embedded part in Test Container has been selected for resizing. The active part in Figure 5-5 is the outer container (the document); within it, the embedded container has been selected so that it can be resized. It is important to note that the embedded part is not active and that the resizing is done by its container (although some negotiation will take place in order for the container and the embedded part to come to terms as to the appropriate size and shape involved).

Embedding Bitmapped Graphics in a Part

As you saw in the previous discussion of Figure 5-4, the address consists of three Text Editor parts embedded in a Test Container part. Most OpenDoc containers are not picky about what they contain—that's the whole point. In the ODF SDK, there's a small example part called ODFBitmap. All it does is allow you to paste a bitmapped graphic into it and to do some basic manipulations with it. Why not add a corporate logo to the mailing label by dragging an ODFBitmap part into the container, as shown in Figure 5-6?

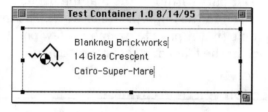

Figure 5-6.

Mailing label with ODFBitmap

When the labels are printed, the mailing label document will continue to request that each part draw itself. The container for this label now contains four parts—three lines of text in Text Editor parts and one graphic in an ODFBitmap part. That change is of no significance to the document.

Editing Embedded Parts

Much of what has been shown here could be accomplished in traditional applications by using cut-and-paste (provided the application supports cutting and pasting of bitmapped graphics as well as text and the application has the rigid formatting required of labels). Remember that OpenDoc goes beyond the simple transfer of data when parts are embedded within one another: The functionality of each part moves along with its data.

Thus, in Figure 5-7, you can see the two address parts discussed in this chapter, one with the corporate logo and one without. The Test Container part used to contain each address has some minimal functionality beyond its ability to embed other parts. This consists of the ability to change its background color. In Figure 5-7, you can see the second address part with its background color is gray. Note that this editing was done within the mailing list document. When the second address part is active (note the activation highlight around the part), its Part Editor claims the menu bar, and the "Change Background Color" menu is able to be used from within the mailing labels document.

In Figure 5-8, a more deeply embedded part is edited. One of the Text Editor parts that is embedded within the Test Container has

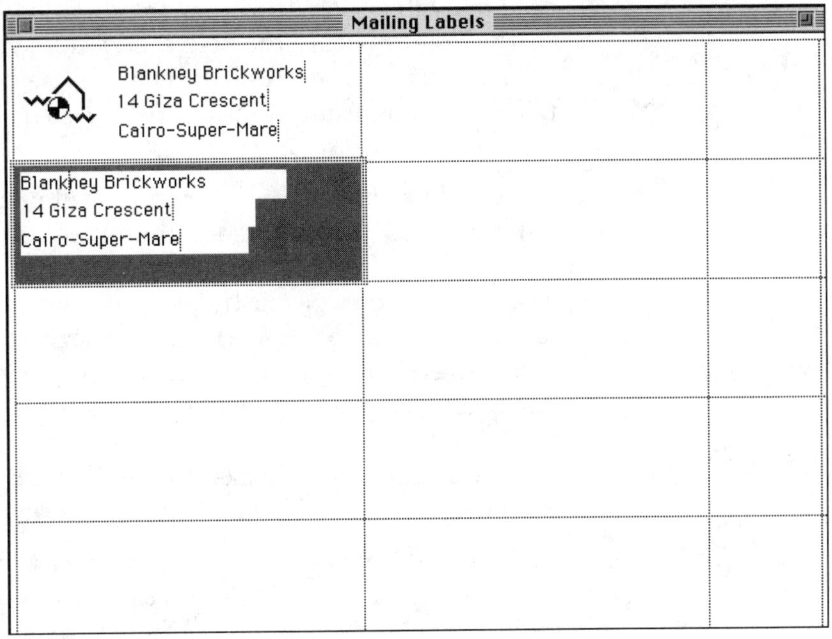

Figure 5-7.

Changing the background color of an embedded part

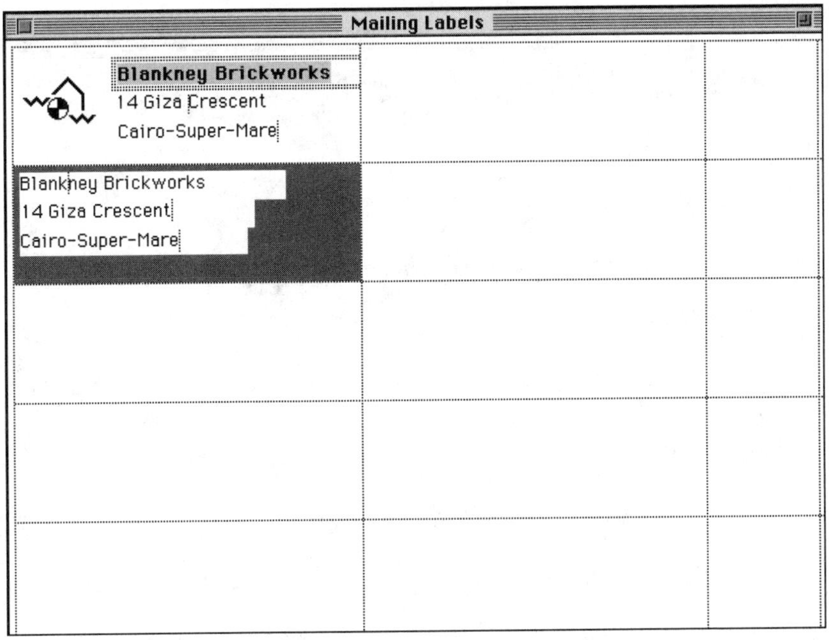

Figure 5-8.

Changing the type style of an embedded text part

been activated (note the activation highlight around "Blankney Brickworks"). Within the activated part, some or all of its content is selected. In this case, all of the data has been selected, and the Bold command from the Style menu has been chosen in order to boldface "Blankney Brickworks."

The ODFBitmap example part that contains the logo is activated in Figure 5-9. One of its menu commands allows you to resize it to 50/100/200% of actual size. In Figure 5-9, the 50% command has been chosen. (It is interesting to note that in its implementation, the ODFBitmap example changes its frame according to the size of the image. Although normally the resizing of embedded parts is handled by the containing part, there are cases such as this where the embedded part may want to change its request for space within the container. In both cases, OpenDoc arbitrates between the container and embedded part as they jostle for space.)

After the bitmapped graphic has been resized, the text of the address appears to be too far to the right. Figure 5-10 shows the embedded address part (containing three further embedded Text Editor parts) after it has been moved slightly to the left.

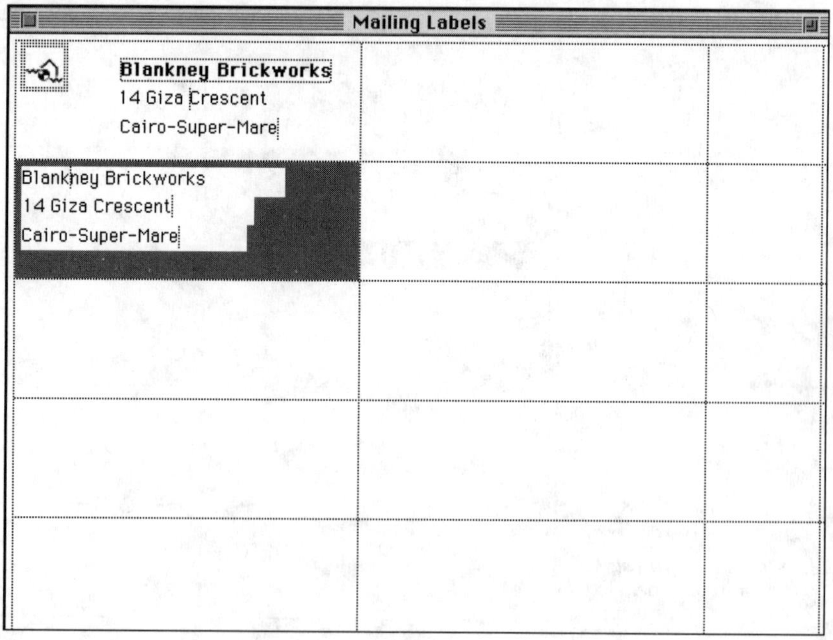

Figure 5-9.
Scaling an embedded bitmap graphic

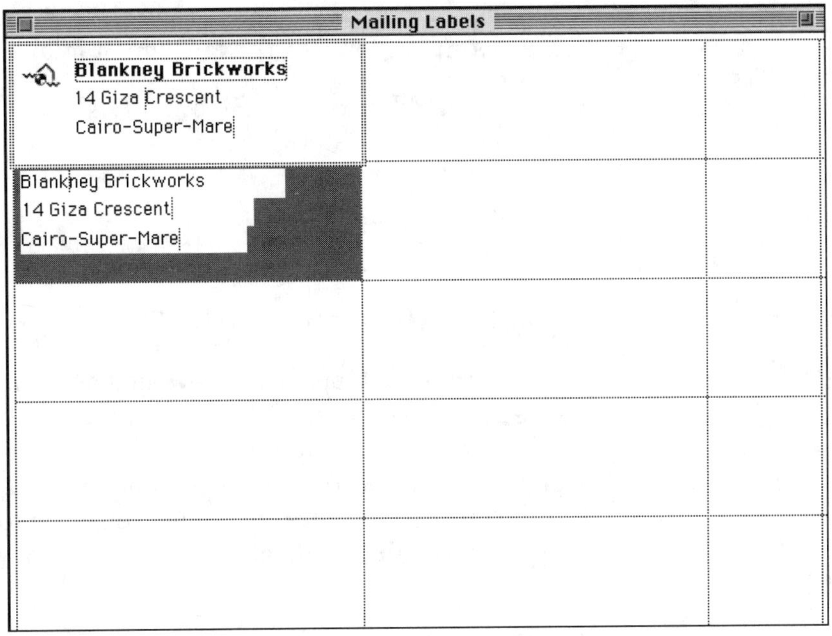

Figure 5-10.

*Moving an
embedded part*

Mailing List Solution—Other Possibilities

The example given here is noteworthy because it is not only quite simple, but also it is very ordinary. The challenge of printing a series of addresses on specially sized labels is one that has stymied people for many years—with typewriters as well as with computers. This is not an example designed to show off the fancy multimedia features of OpenDoc. Rather it is as plain and ordinary a case study as you could want. The incremental enhancements to the task are logical and meaningful to ordinary people. A reasonable person might well want to do these things.

Think now of the application programs with which you are familiar. You probably have a number of large, traditional applications lurking on your hard disk(s). Which could handle the constraints of the label formatting, the full-featured text editing, the inclusion of bitmapped graphics, and the specific positioning of all elements exactly where you want them? Could that 4MB word processor (which needs at least that much memory to run) do it? How about that page layout application, which weighs in at only 3MB (although it's happiest running in about an 8MB partition)?

By comparison, consider the code sizes of the Part Editors used in the example shown in the following table:

Part Editor	Size On Disk
ODFTable	68K
Container	187K
Text Editor	434K
ODFBmp	68K
TOTAL	**757K**

The purpose of OpenDoc is revealed again in these statistics: The OpenDoc shell provides the basic functionality on which all parts rely. Each part, limited in its scope and functionality, includes only its needed code. While implementing OpenDoc's functionality, its developers were extremely sensitive to the bloated disk and memory requirements of most contemporary applications.

You may wonder about OpenDoc's own requirements for memory and disk space. These vary by platform as well as by machine. Development releases of OpenDoc (as with all software) were not optimized for performance, disk, or memory requirements; accordingly, the statistics given here may vary significantly from final performance characteristics. A typical installation of OpenDoc 1.0 Release 3 on a Power Macintosh 8100/80 AV (Power PC 601 chip running at 80 Mhz) required 1.7MB of disk storage for OpenDoc libraries; the runtime OpenDoc shared libraries used about 1.1MB of RAM. Each opened document requires, by default, 768KB of memory. The mailing label "application" described here thus takes about 2.5MB of disk storage and requires 1.8MB of memory to run. Other OpenDoc processes share the OpenDoc libraries, so the incremental "cost" of another solution of the size of the mailing list program, is the approximately 750KB of disk space and 768KB of RAM attributable only to the OpenDoc document in question.

Compare this method of producing mailing labels with other tools such as existing mailing label applications (if you can find one with the formatting functionality described here) or with desktop publishing packages. You will note that the OpenDoc solution is not only streamlined with regard to system requirements; it also is streamlined with regard to the user interface. Your word processor or desktop publishing program may well have a menu command that lets you create an index or table of contents. You don't need such a command for mailing labels, and it is not to be found in the solution given herein. This streamlining is the natural result of focusing on people and their activities. So is the corresponding small footprint for the software as it runs and the minimal training requirements for its use.

Mailing List Solution—Perspectives from Users, Solution Providers, and Developers

The process of creating a mailing list solution has been described here from the user's point of view. It is quite similar for solution providers and developers. In each case, the focus is on a simple activity, on the logical consequences of it, and on the things that can make the process easier, simpler, or more useful.

The solution provider can use even the small number of OpenDoc parts available today to pull together custom solutions of significant power. The domain-specific knowledge of the solution provider (terminology, what exactly it is that users may want to do) makes it possible to pull together simple, powerful parts such as those used here into an extremely valuable solution for clients.

Similarly, the developer of a shrink-wrapped product can move from concept to realization much more quickly by combining parts such as these into a targeted application.

The process is the same in all cases. Start from a basic activity, one that usually can be described quite simply to someone with little knowledge of computers. And then follow it through, stopping to examine logical choices and added features. Even the initial version of OpenDoc ships with several text editors (such as a demo of OpenDoc and a demo of ODF, as well as several third-party versions). Because each part is a fairly limited piece of functionality, the user, solution provider, or developer can choose from among similar parts, mixing and matching them to provide an optimal solution for a specific problem.

A Stroll Through the OpenDoc Libraries

OpenDoc is implemented as part of the system software; there is
no OpenDoc application for users to run and no visible OpenDoc
process for users to see. OpenDoc is not a framework like MacApp,
TCL (Think Class Library), PowerPoint, or MFC (Microsoft Foundation Classes). Instead it is a set of classes that you can instantiate, override, or use to implement your part's functionality.

OpenDoc Subsystems (Shared Libraries)

The set of OpenDoc classes is distributed as a group of shared
libraries, each of which is a subsystem that provides specific functionality to OpenDoc. Each shared library can easily be replaced
with another to provide machine- or platform-specific performance features and enhancements.

The libraries centralize the basic OpenDoc classes that provide
subsystem-level services such as storage, imaging, layout, messaging, scripting support, user interface, memory management,
and various utilities. You need to be concerned with the individual subsystems if you are going to modify them—and you modify
them only if you are provided a new or improved implementation
of OpenDoc on a given platform. To most readers of this book, it is
irrelevant which subsystem implements which OpenDoc classes,
so no more will be said about the specific shared libraries that
support OpenDoc.

OpenDoc Classes

While the OpenDoc library structure is of little concern to users
and OpenDoc developers, the basic OpenDoc classes implemented in the libraries are of major concern to developers (and indirectly to users). The classes are described fully in the *OpenDoc
Class Reference*. This is a 1000-page document that perhaps one
day will be used as a text in computer science curricula that
explore the design and development of software. (OpenDoc is
very well designed and can serve as an exemplar of good object-
oriented software.)

The classes described here are some of the most important of the OpenDoc classes (but by no means all of them). This section is designed to give you a feel for the types of functionality provided by the basic OpenDoc libraries—the functionality available to all OpenDoc parts.

SOM, the system that manages OpenDoc objects at runtime across networks and among various applications, is described in Chapter 6. Some SOM terminology must of necessity creep into this chapter—OpenDoc classes are certainly eggs of the SOM chicken—but SOM is discussed in length later. For the sake of clarity, some of the examples in this chapter have been simplified; they should be taken as pseudo-code rather than the actual API. The most obvious aspect of SOM in this context is the direction keyword—in, out, or inout—that precedes parameters passed to methods.

ODObject

All OpenDoc classes are based on ODObject. It has eight methods and supports the most pervasive OpenDoc concepts. You can see what matters in OpenDoc by looking at the ODObject methods. They fall into three categories:

1. Initialization and Memory Management.

As anyone who has used object-oriented frameworks knows, initialization (or the lack thereof) as well as memory management are the banes of all programmers—although why in this day and age we should still have to rely on manual methods to accomplish these tasks is a mystery. Still, all OpenDoc ODObject classes support the following methods:

```
void InitObject ();
```

InitObject performs initialization for the ODObject.

```
ODSize Purge (in ODSize size);
```

Purge requests the ODObject to release unneeded memory (one hopes in the amount of the size parameter) so that other OpenDoc activities can take place. The amount of memory actually released (if any) is returned in the return value.

2. *Utilities.*

Two utility methods are provided in ODObject. One is used primarily for diagnostics; the other is used frequently in production.

```
void SubClassResponsibility ();
```

This utility posts an exception. It is used in descendants of ODObject as the body of methods that must be overridden by descendants. The error posted is the constant kODErrSub-ClassResponsibility.

```
ODBoolean IsEqualTo (in ODObject object);
```

A descendant of ODObject can decide whether it will be equal to another object. This utility function avoids the need for unsightly attempts to find out if the storage locations of two objects are identical.

3. *Extensions.*

The last three methods of ODObject refer to extensions. Anything in OpenDoc can be extended—even OpenDoc itself. Extensions, which are always descendants of ODExtension, are associated with appropriate OpenDoc objects and are supported by SOM code. It was not an idle boast at the beginning of this book that OpenDoc was planned for extensibility. Here it is, delivered as part of each ODObject.

```
ODBoolean HasExtension (
     in ODType extensionName);
```

You can inquire of any ODObject whether it has a given extension. This method performs that feat. Note that it relies on a parameter of a global type (ODType). Hence objects that have long since been compiled and released into production can easily respond to requests as to whether they have a given extension, which may have been designed and implemented years after the base object.

```
ODExtension AcquireExtension (
     in ODType extensionName);
```

If an object has an extension, you may need to obtain a reference to it in order to use it. At this time, ODObject class has no extensions, and this method always posts the kODErrUnsupportedExtension for the ODObject class. For other classes, it will either post the exception or return a reference to the extension object.

```
void ReleaseExtension (in ODExtension extension);
```

If you obtained a reference to an extension with AcquireExtension, you release it with this method. Calls to AcquireExtension should be balanced by calls to Release.

ODExtension

The ODExtension object itself is an abstract superclass that provides the basic extension hooks to OpenDoc, as described immediately above.

Non OpenDoc extensions, such as the generic text engine used in the Text Editor example and shown at ❶, can be integrated easily into the OpenDoc world. This style facilitates OpenDoc coordination and integration with existing systems.

```
SOM_Scope void  SOMLINK TextEditor__DoCopy(
    SampleCode_TextEditor *somSelf,
    Environment *ev,
    ODFrame* frame)
{
    SampleCode_TextEditorData *somThis =
SampleCode_TextEditorGetData(somSelf);
    TOffsetRange curSelectionRange;
    ❷ ODSession*session = somSelf->
GetStorageUnit(ev)->GetSession(ev);
    ODDraft* fromDraft = somSelf->
GetStorageUnit(ev)->GetDraft(ev);


    // Acquire clipboard focus
    ❹ session->GetArbitrator(ev)->
RequestFocus(ev, gClipboardFocus, frame);
```

```
// Get the selection range to be written out.
❶ _fTextension->GetSelectionRange
(&curSelectionRange);

❸ ODClipboard* clipboard = session
->GetClipboard(ev);
```

. . .

This section of code has references to a number of other basic OpenDoc classes.

ODSession

At ❷, you see a reference to the ODSession object that is being obtained through the storage unit (definition coming up; hold your horses). The session object is a critical runtime object in OpenDoc, mediating between a given document and the OpenDoc class libraries. The ODSession object is created by the document shell. Part editors never create ODSession objects, although they frequently need to refer to them.

At ❸, you see an example of the ODSession object's being asked to provide a reference to one of its objects. These are objects that are shared by parts and thus have meaning at the document level. They are not parts of the document *per se*, but are runtime constructs that make the management of the document possible. The object being found at ❸ is the clipboard, perhaps the most obvious example of an object that has meaning beyond the level of the individual part.

There are 15 ODSession objects. Three in particular give an added feel for the way in which OpenDoc functions: the **arbitrator**, the **dispatcher**, and the **undo stack**.

ODArbitrator

The ODSession's arbitrator manages temporary ownership of resources (such as the menu bar) and events (keystrokes) that must be linked to a single part handler. Part editors request **foci,** that is, temporary ownership of these shared resources, from the

ODArbitrator before gaining access to these resources and events, which could possibly by wanted by other parts.

In the discussion of the processes shown in the figures earlier in this chapter, you saw that a part could be activated with a mouse click and then directly manipulated. In fact, the sequence is as follows:

1. You select the contents of a frame (usually by clicking in it).

2. The part that owns the frame activates it and requests the foci so that it owns the appropriate shared resources. There is a specific focus for the menu bar, another for the keystrokes, another for selection, and still another for resources such as a communications port. At ❹ in the previous code sample, you can see the part editor requesting the arbitrator from the session and then requesting the clipboard focus from the arbitrator for the active frame (the ODFrame parameter frame).

Foci are generally owned exclusively; for example, only one part at a time usually gets keystrokes. But there are cases where nonexclusive ownership is required. OpenDoc supports this form of ownership.

The methods of the ODArbitrator object thus are entirely related to foci. You can request foci (as in the example at ❹ above), transfer them to another owner if you know what that will be, or relinquish them so that the ODArbitrator can give them to another part editor for its active frame.

Further, you can create sets of foci that can then be requested, transferred, and relinquished in the same way individual foci can.

ODDispatcher

The ODDispatcher object manages the sending of events to a given part editor. In traditional applications, the application polls the operating system to find out what events have occurred that it may want to process (the main event loop). In OpenDoc the shell does this polling and passes all the events to the dispatcher. Part editors respond only to events received from the dispatcher; the main event loop is hidden from the parts inside the OpenDoc Session.

The implementation of event dispatching is the most platform-specific part of OpenDoc. (Drawing to the screen is a close second.) One of the major tasks of an operating system is the management of system resources and user interaction. Each operating system takes a different (sometimes radically different) approach to these issues. So, OpenDoc's shared libraries implement event dispatching quite differently for each platform, although by the time events actually come down to a part handler, they are largely platform-neutral.

You will rarely need to deal with the ODDispatcher object directly, although every time you do anything to an OpenDoc document the ODDispatcher object constantly interacts with the session and the operating system (and through it, the user). There are two aspects of the dispatcher that you may need to be aware of and one item of passing interest.

Last things first: The item of passing interest is that the dispatcher has the call that closes a document:

```
void Exit ();
```

The container application and document shell often call ShouldExit to see if the dispatcher recommends that the main event loop be terminated:

```
ODBoolean ShouldExit ();
```

Routing Events

The routing of events to part handlers is actually a two-step process. The dispatcher contains references to ODDispatchModule objects, which are associated with specific events. When an event is presented to the dispatcher (via the Dispatch method), it looks up that event in its tables to find an ODDispatchModule that is associated with it. If it finds an ODDispatchModule, it passes the event on to it. The ODDispatchModule then calls the appropriate part's HandleEvent method.

This structure is used commonly in OpenDoc. Many object-oriented applications change the behavior of their main event-handling objects by overriding them. Thus traditional object-oriented applications are characterized by overrides of their application object's most basic functionality (this, after all, is what object-oriented programming is about).

In the style used here, the basic class is generally not overriden. Instead, it contains intrinsic hooks that allow for overriding. ODObject is designed to handle extensions. ODDispatch is designed to handle various ODDispatch-Modules that provide modifications of behavior that in other structures might have been achieved by overriding an ODDispatch class.

This design is not arbitrary and capricious. Rather, it represents an appropriate response to one of the most serious difficulties encountered in developing object-oriented applications.

Adding Modules to Manage Events

If you need to add dispatch modules to manage events, this trio of ODDispatch methods are helpful:

```
void AddDispatchModule (
    in ODEventType eventType,
    in ODDispatchModule dispatchModule);
```

This method associates the given module with the event type specified in the first parameter.

To reverse the process, call

```
void RemoveDispatchModule (
    in ODEventType eventType);
```

And if you need to get your hands on a given dispatch module, you can call

```
ODDispatchModule GetDispatchModule (
    in ODEventType eventType);
```

Part editors rarely change the dispatch modules in the dispatcher. These calls are shown here only to illustrate the structure and to show the extensibility of OpenDoc.

A more likely (but still infrequent) modification to the dispatch object is the installation of monitors, that is, dispatch modules that monitor the event stream without touching it. You can install a monitor for certain event types in order to trace events. You can then dispatch the event off to the original (real) dispatch module.

ODUndo

The last ODSession object that will be examined here is the Undo stack. It manages the multilevel undo feature of OpenDoc. This feature allows users to repeat a number of actions. Clearly it can easily involve several different parts, and only the OpenDoc session has the capability to handle this situation.

Nevertheless, it is worth examining the structure of the ODUndo object, since it shows clearly OpenDoc's capabilities in this area. Historically, the Undo command has been tremendously important in the growth of graphical user interfaces. When properly designed, applications provide undo capabilities for virtually anything that you might do. The consequence of this is that users are far less frightened of their computers. They try things out and see what will happen, secure in the knowledge that any damage can easily be undone.

Like many simple features of computer applications, undo quickly ran up against the complexity of the users and their activities. Users would do something of significance that they might want to undo. Then, without thinking, they would go on and do something trivial that also could be undone. Lo and behold, the trivial command became the command that could be undone, and when the user tried to undo the significant command (perhaps a Delete All command), it was no longer undoable.

Context-sensitive undo and undo stacks were proposed as solutions to this problem. Context-sensitive undo allows the user to undo the previous action (still usually only one) for each window or document in an application. This logical feature did not sweep the software development world by storm. As a result users often did not know it existed and developers became even less eager to use it. With Undo behaving in nonstandard (and even unpredictable) ways, users became less willing to rely on the feature, and developers were less rigorous about including it in their applications. (Examine the applications you regularly use to see how Undo is implemented. You will probably be surprised at its inconsistent implementation—and even its absence—in many cases.)

Undo stacks provide the ability to undo a whole sequence of actions and so would appear to solve many of the interface and behavioral issues associated with Undo. It's not nirvana, however. It is easy for a user to accumulate a whole list of actions to be undone—and be left befuddled trying to remember what the fifth previous Move Shape command actually was all about.

OpenDoc's implementation of Undo is based on a marked Undo stack. Actions are added to the stack by parts as they are done; enough information is provided by the part so that the part can identify the action and redo it if necessary. Further, the part provides the appropriate text for the menu to use in displaying the command. (Some frameworks carefully construct the Undo or Redo menu item from the wording of the original command. OpenDoc asks that the part provide the actual text rather than trying to construct it. This solved a number of problems that arose as peculiarly worded items were generated for the Undo command. It also makes localization into non-English languages easier.)

In fact, the ODUndo object has two stacks: one for Undo commands and one for Redo commands. They move in parallel. The eight methods of ODUndo, discussed next, show how the functionality is achieved.

The major method of ODUndo is AddActionToHistory. Parts call this method to log an undoable action to ODUndo.

```
void AddActionToHistory (
     in ODPart whichPart,
     in ODActionData actionData,
     in ODActionType actionType,
     in ODName undoActionLabel,
     in ODName redoActionLabel);
```

If a part is logging its actions directly (rarely the case if you are using a framework like ODF), it would obtain the session's Undo object in a call similar to the one above in which the arbitrator was obtained:

```
ODUndo undo = session->GetUndo(ev);
```

The actionData parameter is an ODPtr structure (a pointer) into which the part places all the information it will need to redo the action. The actionType parameter may have any of the following values:

```
kODSingleAction
```

```
kODBeginAction
```

```
kODEndAction
```

These values allow a part to place complex actions onto the Undo stack. The final two parameters are the strings that OpenDoc will use in the menubar.

Parts can mark the Undo stack so that a series of actions can be manipulated together. A part marks the Undo stack by calling MarkActionHistory:

```
void MarkActionHistory ();
```

This routine simply marks the current tops of the Undo and Redo stacks.

Thereafter a part can clear the stacks by calling ClearAction-History:

```
void ClearActionHistory (
    in ODRespectMarksChoices respectMarks);
```

Two constants are defined for ODRespectMarksChoices:

```
kODRespectMarks
```

```
KODDontRespectMarks
```

If the first is used, the Undo stack is cleared down to the last marked action; in the second case, the stack is completely cleared.

A comparable method clears the Redo stack and always respects the action history:

```
void ClearRedoHistory ();
```

Because the Undo and Redo stacks are maintained by the session (that is, at the document level), occasionally a part may need to check to see what the current status is. The top of each stack is visible with these two methods:

```
ODBoolean PeekUndoHistory (
     out ODPart part,
     out ODActionData actionData,
     out ODActionType, actionType,
     out ODName actionLabel);
ODBoolean PeekRedoHistory (
     out ODPart part,
     out ODActionData actionData,
     out ODActionType, actionType,
     out ODName actionLabel);
```

The parameters are similar to those of AddActionToHistory. The return value for each method has the value kODTrue if a history item was found on the top of the appropriate stack.

The actual undoing and redoing are generated by the document that calls the following two methods as needed:

```
void Undo ();
void Redo ();
```

Unless you are writing an OpenDoc document shell (as opposed to a part), you do not call these methods directly.

The ODUndo class performs vital management for the OpenDoc interface. In its methods as shown here, you can see its architecture and power, as well as its simplicity. In contrast to object-oriented frameworks, OpenDoc has a very simple structure, with minimized inheritance. Classes are quite independent, and developers rarely need to access OpenDoc classes or methods themselves.

There is, however, a slight degree of inheritance in the OpenDoc structure. All objects descend from ODObject. Independent run-time objects simply subclass ODObject. Examples of these classes are the facet class (used to display information and quickly respond to mouse clicks); the session, undo, and arbitrator objects described earlier in the chapter, and other objects that serve special purposes.

Some objects are shared among a number of parts or other objects. To maintain the integrity of those objects, OpenDoc needs to know how many other objects refer to them. A subclass of ODObject, ODRefCntObject, provides this information.

ODRefCntObject

An ODRefCntObject is typically shared during an OpenDoc session. Several OpenDoc objects have references to it, so it cannot be deleted by one object without adversely affecting those other objects. Examples of such runtime shared objects are the menu bar, containers, documents, drafts (i.e., versions of documents), and windows. These objects all descend from ODRefCntObject, which has these four methods:

```
void InitRefCntObject ();

void Acquire ();

void Release ();

ODLong GetRefCount ();
```

These methods, respectively, initialize the object, increment its reference count by 1, decrement its reference count by 1, and return the current reference count.

This method of managing referential integrity at runtime is common in many applications and databases. It is a robust way of managing shared resources, provided everyone plays by the rules. Descendants of ODRefCntObject are normally created in only a few places in OpenDoc, so this scheme works well.

As part of this look at OpenDoc, it is important to point out that managing runtime integrity of shared objects is not an add-on. It is an intrinsic part of OpenDoc and is one of the features that makes it so powerful.

While the reference count method is common for managing runtime-shared objects, much more control is needed for objects that are needed across different OpenDoc sessions. For these objects, a subclass of ODRefCntObject exists: ODPersistentObject.

ODPersistentObject

Like other aspects of OpenDoc, this class is quite simple. Its responsibilities (and associated methods) are few, easy to understand, and powerful. Because OpenDoc is centered around documents that traditionally are closely related to files on personal computers, it is not unreasonable to assume that OpenDoc is very concerned with storage and the saving of documents. If you have followed the technical journals and discussion groups devoted to object-oriented programming since the mid-1980s, you likely have noticed the amount of time devoted to the discussion of persistent objects. It has always been relatively easy to create an object at runtime. In order to re-create it later, however, you need not only the physical data storage systems, but also a way to re-create any runtime structures that were created when the object was first instantiated.

Many object-oriented frameworks assume data storage is a customization of objects and that the application developer will handle input and output specifically for any given application that is constructed. In retrospect, many people believe an inordinate amount of time is thus spent reinventing many wheels in order to provide storage and retrieval of runtime objects.

OpenDoc does not have a choice when it comes to object persistence. Because it is a document-centered architecture, it must manage storage, input, and output, all of which it does with ODPersistentObject and its descendants.

There are eight methods of ODPersistentObject. The first two are simple initialization routines:

```
void InitPersistentObject (
    in ODStorageUnit storageUnit);
void InitPersistentObjectFromStorage(
    in ODStorageUnit storageUnit);
```

The first initializes a newly created object; the second initializes an object from stored data. Note that both methods require a storage unit parameter. All persistent objects must have a storage unit associated with them, even if they have not yet been saved.

(Storage units are discussed in Chapter 7, "Managing OpenDoc Files and Storage: the Container Suite.")

Objects may be moved to storage either because they are being written to disk or because they are temporarily being cached somewhere, perhaps in response to a request made through the ODObject Purge method. This routine must be subclassed for each ODPersistentObject, but its prototype is

```
void Externalize ();
```

Remember that each ODPersistentObject has a storage unit associated with it at initialization time, thus the Externalize method knows where to put the object. At times you will need to know what a part's storage unit is. In those cases, you can call

```
ODStorageUnit GetStorageUnit ();
```

If you are externalizing an object in order to write it to disk and be done with it, you need to make certain that all references from it to other objects are released. This will prevent the reference count of other objects from remaining artificially high with "ghosts" holding on to them.

The ReleaseAll method

```
void ReleaseAll ();
```

takes care of releasing all references from the ODPersistentObject to others. This is normally not called directly from your code; it is called by the object that created the persistent object.

Two other methods which provide very important functionality to ODPersistentObject classes. The first

```
ODID GetID();
```

you can use to get a unique identifier for this object. This identifier is not persistent; it is unique for a given draft of a document and a given session (i.e., it is unique at runtime).

The second lets you copy an object somewhere else:

```
void CloneInto (
    in ODDraftKey key,
    in ODStorageUnit toSU,
    in ODFrame scope);
```

This routine (which you call indirectly during a cloning operation) lets you clone an object into a storage unit. Objects to which it has strong persistent references are cloned as well, if they are within the scope (a frame) specified in the third parameter. If the scope is kODNULL, all such objects are also cloned. (Note, this routine is presented here only for the sake of completeness of the list of ODPersistentObject methods.)

In this brief overview, you have seen some of the features and architecture of OpenDoc. Most of these classes are never subclassed in part editors; many of these routines are never called directly. They are part of the OpenDoc libraries and provide its functionality and features.

One class, however, is different: ODPart.

ODPart

ODPart must be subclassed and its methods overridden by every part editor. Your override of ODPart serves as the basis of your part editor. ODPart has 60 methods, and you must override each of them. This is not as a daunting a task as it might appear at first. Some of the methods implement functionality that may not apply to your part. In such cases, a stub implementation that does nothing is sufficient. Furthermore, if you use a framework such as ODF or a tool such as PartMaker, the methods—with stubs and/or basic functionalities—will be created for you automatically.

Frameworks have become essential tools in the creation of software. As the complexity of software increased, and the time to develop and test software grew at least proportionately, developers struggled to find ways to reduce these staggering costs. In the late 1980s, object-oriented programming held out a promise of relief. It appeared then that objects could be created, tested, and then incorporated into various applications. Code reuse, one of the Holy Grails of programming, came into sight. Unfortunately, for many years it remained just beyond reach.

Object-oriented programming didn't fail; in fact, it is more alive today than it has ever been. But in retrospect, it seems clear that the idea of reusable objects was an overly optimistic, perhaps even simplistic, goal, given the absence of an environment such as OpenDoc. OpenDoc addresses the problems that people encountered with reusing objects. Its parts are true objects, and very highly structured ones. They are reusable, and usable in many contexts, because of the rules they must obey. There is a relatively long list of messages that each OpenDoc part must be able to reply to or to act on. This structured environment makes the reuse of OpenDoc parts the reality that less structured object-oriented objects were rarely able to achieve.

Within a part's implementation, however, OpenDoc's rules are practically nonexistent. How a part responds to an OpenDoc request is up to the part. How the code is written is not Open-Doc's business. The personal, even idiosyncratic, code styles of different companies and programmers can be given free reign within OpenDoc parts. As examples distributed with OpenDoc show, you can even write part editors in a non-object-oriented-language, and no one will be the wiser.

Programming today is akin to piloting the most modern airplanes which are so complex that they must be flown by computer with the pilot only indirectly manipulating the mechanical controls. Few programmers would attempt to work without an integrated development environment and an object-oriented framework. To prove this point (and because this chapter is long enough), here is the essential guide to ODPart:

1. You must subclass ODPart and override each of its methods (with stubs in the case of functionality you don't care about).

2. When you use a framework like ODF, most of this is done for you.

3. The discussion of what you have to do to implement a part is deferred to Chapter 16, "OpenDoc Development Framework," which describes ODF in some detail.

Summary

This chapter is obviously a very high-level, cursory overview of the OpenDoc runtime structure. Nevertheless, you should find it sufficient to provide you with a context in which to look at how parts function within OpenDoc. The internal structures of

OpenDoc are discussed in more detail later in the book, but be warned—these are discussed primarily from the point of view of parts and their editors. Just as many people find it interesting to examine the innards of operating systems, there are many people who are curious about just exactly how OpenDoc works. For those who are morbidly curious about the innards of OpenDoc, the source code is available from CI Labs. Many more people, however, are satisfied to take OpenDoc as the functional entity that it is and to worry about the things over which they have control—the parts they can use and the part editors they can write. For these people, the very brief summary in this chapter provides enough of an insight into OpenDoc. In-depth studies can then be devoted to parts themselves.

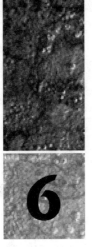

6

Managing OpenDoc Objects: SOM

In Chapter 5, you saw a very high-level view of OpenDoc's technology. In this chapter and the two that follow, you will explore three of the technologies that support OpenDoc's functionality. In this chapter, the System Object Model (SOM), which enables OpenDoc's parts and components to work together at runtime, is described. Without SOM, OpenDoc simply wouldn't work. It's reassuring to know that if you're an end-user of OpenDoc, you need never know about SOM, and that as a developer or designer of OpenDoc parts and containers, you likely will never need to touch SOM directly, thanks to the integrated development environments, frameworks, and development tools that do the work for you.

In the next chapter, OpenDoc's storage mechanism is described. Users may not need to become overly familiar with it, but developers and designers usually do need to know something about it and will need to study that chapter.

Following that, OpenDoc's Open Scripting Architecture (OSA) is described in Chapter 8. OSA is relevant to users as well as to developers and designers. It is particularly interesting to systems integrators, value-added resellers, and consultants who are creating custom solutions.

If you are willing to take on faith that OpenDoc just works, and if you don't particularly care how it works, feel free to skip this chapter. But if you have any doubts about whether you can believe the near-miracles that OpenDoc promises with regard to assembling software, this chapter is essential. As you saw with the ODObject class in the last chapter, OpenDoc's major functionalities were included in the design from the start.

Making Connections Among Objects and Code at Runtime—The Problem

Once programs became more than a few lines long, people started to try to reuse the code in them. The natural human inclination to combine familiar tools in new ways to create new machines and processes flourished from the dawn of the Computer Age, usually despite the incredible difficulties encountered in the attempts.

IMS and Its Gens

In the late 1970s and early 1980s, Rockwell International developed the IMS software for IBM mainframes. IMS was a remarkable system. In many ways, its design presaged a number of important object-oriented system features. Its applications consisted of a (large) number of (very small) programs. Each program generally did one thing and then handed control off to another program. The formatted data entry screens on IBM 3270 terminals were often programmed with IMS screen programs. System development was logically quite simple. A data entry screen was designed and copies of it circulated for comments. Users and developers corrected misspellings, changed the order of data entry fields, and generally modified the screen design until they were happy. Programmers took the revised screen design and wrote a simple program to retrieve the data from each field, validate it, and then pass it on to another process.

Modular, reusable software seemed to have arrived. Need a name/address data entry screen and program for your payroll program? All you would have to do is take the name/address data entry screen from the customer account program and change the title, and presto! You've got your payroll data entry.

If IMS or something like it had existed in this form, OpenDoc likely wouldn't exist today. The paradigms of computing would be quite different. Mainframes may have retained a much more prominent role in the computing world of the 1990s. And desktop computers likely would have retained many more features of mainframe operating systems.

Unfortunately, IMS, although a truly innovative, creative, and wonderful design, was implemented with a few unpleasant "gotchas." Many developers and designers who were enthusiastic after the first half-day of an introductory IMS class were discouraged to learn after lunch that all the really elegant features of the system and of its database structure were generally declared off-limits in most installations for reasons of performance. What was left was a collection of interesting features with a very tantalizing set of verboten features that, if used, would (supposedly) reduce the system to a crawl.

And there was another "gotcha": Gens. Programmers who worked on mainframes in the mid-1970s to mid-1980s knew all about Gens. So did their families, their friends, and their neighborhood liquor store owners. For all of the elegant little IMS programs to work together, the system had to be *generated* (hence "Gen"). This system generation collected all of the pieces and indexed and ordered them appropriately. It also made it possible for one screen program to hand off its data to another program or to a database. The individual programs were reasonably encapsulated, but the system had to know about everything. And for the system to know about everything that happened in its entire IMS world, a Gen had to take place. With few exceptions, any change of any significance to any IMS program required the system to be re-Genned. For example, a modification to a payroll program that ran under IMS on a mainframe often meant the warehouse management program that ran in the same IMS on that same mainframe had to be re-Genned, as did the accounting software, the customer database, and so on.

Gens could fail, and in most installations a representative from each of the major production systems was on call (or on site!) during the Gen in case something untoward happened. Gens traditionally started after weekly backups were done at the close of business on Friday night (or Saturday morning) and continued as needed, usually into Sunday. (It has never been proven that Gens occurred only on absolutely beautiful weekends or weekends on which fell marriages, birthdays, or other festive events. A case of a Gen being named as a corespondent in a divorce case was widely reported but cannot be verified.)

Object-Oriented Programming's Dirty Little Secret

It would be unfair to blame IMS for Gens; the problem Gens address is common. When pieces of software need to communicate among one another, often sharing data in an intimate manner (as opposed to transferring it in flat files in a common format), keeping track of the connections quickly becomes a mammoth undertaking. When you add the complexity arising from networks, different operating systems, and various computer languages, the problems seem insurmountable. The proponents of object-oriented programming promised much of the modularity and code reuse that was promised by champions of IMS in the old days. There was no need to have Gens on the desktop, but it was still necessary to find some way for these separate pieces of code to establish appropriate relationships.

With object-oriented systems, the solution quickly became to distribute source code for objects and classes and to recompile it in any environment that used it. Thus programmers developing around a framework such as MacApp, TCL, or MFC often needed to recompile the framework in order to subclass its parts and to properly have the objects they wrote reference their superclasses. The goal of being able to subclass an object to which the developer only has the binary code has remained generally just beyond reach.

System Object Model

In the early 1990s, IBM took the bull by the horns and developed the System Object Model. Its goal was to allow runtime binding of objects to one another, no matter in what environment they had been developed. Interlanguage binding would be taken as a given, and classes that existed only in binary code would have to be allowed to be subclassed by client code at runtime. Changes to the implementation of a class would not require its client classes (descendants) to be recompiled, although changes to the interface of such a class might require recompilation of descendants. (Adding methods or instance variables generally does not require such recompilation unless the descendant uses the new methods or variables.)

The major goal of SOM is to allow people to create and use objects that are descendants (or subclasses) of other objects, just as in traditional object-oriented programming. However, the parent objects are available only in binary form, and modifications to the parent object to the greatest extent possible do not require modifications or recompilation of the descendants. In part of the SOM specification, the Distributed System Object Model (DSOM) is introduced. DSOM takes the abstraction one level further: The parent object may be running in another process, possibly on another machine. A call to an inherited method may wind up executing across a network.

Another important feature of SOM is its language neutrality. You can invoke SOM routines from object-oriented languages like C++ just as you can from procedural languages such as C. If you have been around the world of software development for any period of time, your antennae will likely go up at the mention of "language neutrality." Yes, SOM's language neutrality is achieved with those two time-honored means:

1. Yet another language (which is "neutral," as opposed to existing languages, which aren't)
2. A whole bunch of defines and conditional compilation statements

This isn't too terrible. After all, in most cases you never see the SOM code that is inside an OpenDoc part (even if you are the programmer). And when you do, you usually need to only make a minor modification or insert some customized sample code.

Interface Definition Language

The core of SOM from the programmer's point of view is the Interface Definition Language (IDL) in which the objects are described. (PartMaker and other such tools create appropriate

IDL files for your parts.) By convention, each IDL file describes one class. These files are not used directly in the development process but are run through the SOM compiler (see the next section), where language-specific files are produced.

> The Object Management Group is an industry organization that establishes standards with regard to shared objects. They sponsor the Common Object Request Broker Architecture (CORBA), which contains the specifications for the Interface Definition Language. The language discussed here is, technically speaking, SOM IDL—IBM's implementation of IDL for SOM. The extensions to CORBA IDL that SOM IDL supports are noted in the text; in the code samples they are bracketed with conditional compilation commands (_SOMIDL_).

Strictly speaking, the IDL specifies the interface of the objects that will be supported in SOM. This interface will be relatively familiar to C and C++ programmers. C++ programmers will also note that the interface bears a striking similarity to the declaration of a C++ class.

If you run a utility such as PartMaker to create the basic files for a new OpenDoc part, you must provide three pieces of information:

1. An existing OpenDoc part for the utility to use as a template
2. The name of the part you want to create
3. The name of the organization or company creating the part (This name is used not only for documentation purposes but to provide a unique name for the part.)

Starting from the C++ Sample Part, PartMaker created the following IDL file for a part called "DemoPart" for a company called "Philmont Software." Note that the name of the part and the name of the author are used throughout the IDL file—sometimes alone, sometimes as parts of new identifiers ("som_DemoPart"). For this reason, do not use dummy names for your part or company; changing them—even with an intelligent editor—is not easy. The top of the file that is produced has descriptive information

and includes the part.idl file, which contains information about
ODPart. Then follows this code:

```
❶ module PhilmontSoftware
{
    ❷ interface som_DemoPart : ODPart
    {
#ifdef __SOMIDL__
        ❸ implementation
        {
            ❹ functionprefix = som_DemoPart__;
            ❺ override:
                //# ODObject methods
                somInit,
                somUninit,
                AcquireExtension,
                HasExtension,
                Purge,
                ReleaseExtension,

                //# ODRefCountedObject methods
                Release,

                //# ODPersistentObject methods.
                CloneInto,
                Externalize,
                ReleaseAll,

                //# ODPart methods
                AbortRelinquishFocus,
                AcquireContainingPartProperties,
                AdjustBorderShape,
                AdjustMenus,
```

```
AttachSourceFrame,
BeginRelinquishFocus,
CanvasChanged,
CanvasUpdated,
ChangeKind,
ClonePartInfo,
CommitRelinquishFocus,
ContainingPartPropertiesUpdated,
CreateEmbeddedFramesIterator,
CreateLink,
DisplayFrameAdded,
DisplayFrameClosed,
DisplayFrameConnected,
DisplayFrameRemoved,
DisposeActionState,
DragEnter,
DragLeave,
DragWithin,
Draw,
Drop,
DropCompleted,
EditInLinkAttempted,
EmbeddedFrameUpdated,
EmbeddedFrameSpec,
ExternalizeKinds,
FacetAdded,
FacetRemoved,
FocusAcquired,
FocusLost,
FrameShapeChanged,
FulfillPromise,
GeometryChanged,
```

```
                    GetPrintResolution,
                    HandleEvent,
                    HighlightChanged,
                    InitPart,
                    InitPartFromStorage,
                    LinkStatusChanged,
                    LinkUpdated,
                    Open,
                    PresentationChanged,
                    ReadActionState,
                    ReadPartInfo,
                    RedoAction,
                    RemoveEmbeddedFrame,
                    RequestEmbeddedFrame,
                    RequestFrameShape,
                    RevealFrame,
                    RevealLink,
                    SequenceChanged,
                    UndoAction,
                    UsedShapeChanged,
                    ViewTypeChanged,
                    WriteActionState,
                    WritePartInfo;


            ➏ majorversion = 1; minorversion = 0;


➐ #ifdef __PRIVATE__
            ➑ — passthru C_xih =
                "class DemoPart;";


            ➒ DemoPart*        fPart;


#endif //__PRIVATE__
```

```
        };
#endif //__SOMIDL__
    };
};
```

Module Declaration

The module statement at ❶ defines scoping—those interfaces within a module are at the same lexical level. Modules may be nested to provide greater control over the scope of the interfaces and may appear in one IDL file. In most cases, however, one interface/object is defined in each file.

Interface Declaration

The interface declaration starts by declaring the object's class name and identifying its parent class(es), as shown at ❷. In this case, the part is a descendant only of the ODPart.

You can declare constants, types, exceptions, attributes, and methods for your class. In this case, there are none (they only are inherited from the parent class). Constants and types are declarations that are familiar to most programmers. Exceptions, attributes, and methods, however, are IDL declarations that warrant a brief further look.

Exception Declaration

An exception declaration defines data structures that are used when errors occur during a method's execution. It is similar to a struct. It has a name and may contain a number of data elements.

The first parameter of most SOM method calls in C++[†] is an Environment* parameter (usually called "ev"). Recall the following line of code from Chapter 5:

```
session->GetArbitrator(ev)->RequestFocus(ev,
    gClipboardFocus, frame);
```

[†]When called from C, the first parameter of a SOM method is the object and the second is the environment. Thus the C++ code `myObject-->somCall (ev)` is equivalent to the C code `somCall (myObject,ev)`.

The first parameter to both the GetArbitrator and RequestFocus methods is the environment parameter. Within a method, when an error is encountered, you can call somSetException:

```
void somSetException (Environment* ev,

    exception_type major,

    string exception_name,

    void* params);
```

The environment is passed back to the caller who can interrogate it. The exception_type may have the values NO_EXCEPTION, USER_EXCEPTION, or SYSTEM_EXCEPTION. The string is the name of the exception that you define in the IDL file, and the pointer to the parameters is a pointer to a struct that was defined in the exception declaration.

In this way, error-management is built into all SOM method calls. A number of standard exceptions that cover most generally encountered errors are built into SOM.

Attribute Declaration

An attribute is similar to a declaration of a variable, but the SOM compiler automatically generates accessor routines for attributes. Thus, for the part DemoPart, the statement

```
attribute short aShort;
```

would produce definitions of the following methods:

```
short _get_aShort();
```

```
void _set_aShort (in short aShort);
```

Using attributes produces cleaner, more maintainable code. It is also important for distributed programming and values that need to be generated (instead of stored).

In IDL, each parameter is preceded by one of the keywords *in, out,* or *inout* to indicate its use in the method.

Method Declaration

Finally, you may declare methods that are part of this class and that are not overridden or inherited.

Implementation Statement

Returning to the code sample earlier in the chapter, note the implementation statement that starts at ❸. The implementation statement is an extension to the CORBA standard, so it is bracketed with conditional compilation statements that allow its compilation only for SOM.

Each line (terminated by a semicolon) of an implementation may be either a modifier statement, a passthru statement, or an instance variable declaration. They may be present in any order.

For example, at ❹, you see a modifier that sets the SOM-defined value functionprefix to som_DemoPart__. This prefix will be used to construct all procedure names generated by the compiler for this interface, thereby enhancing readability. The value som_DemoPart__ was created by PartMaker based on the name of the part. In the code segment shown later in this chapter, you will see the implementations of methods that have been named with this prefix.

At ❺, the override modifier specifies a list of inherited methods that this class will override. This code segment is given in its entirety so as to show the methods of ODObject, ODRefCounted-Object, ODPersistentObject, and ODPart that each OpenDoc part must implement. (Don't panic. The stubs of these methods are all generated automatically, and normally you need to write code for only a few of them. Obviously, the more complex your part is, the more you need to implement.)

Finally, at ❻ you see the version information that you can specify in an IDL file. When linking code together at runtime, SOM checks that the appropriate versions of classes are matched.

The SOM compiler uses the IDL file to generate interfaces for clients (who need not know anything about the internal structure of a class) as well as for implementors (who do need this information). The conditional compilation statement at ❼ is generated to make certain the following two lines of code are not visible.

The passthru statement at ❽ is used to place the quoted string in a specific file that the SOM compiler generates at a specific location. In this case, when a .xih file is emitted for the C language, this string is placed before the #include statements in the header file. The passthru statement can thus be used to include non-SOM structures in an IDL file.

Finally, note the all-important line of code at ❾. This is the declaration that links your part (DemoPart) to the SOM class (som_DemoPart). The automatically generated methods for your SOM class will use this variable. The SOM class wraps your C or C++ code, so that SOM calls—from wherever—can get to your code's functionality.

SOM Class Implementation

In addition, in the IDL file described previously, PartMaker creates an implementation file with stubs (and sometimes more) for each of the methods you list in the implementation section of your interface. Thus the fact that you have to implement 60 methods for each OpenDoc part should not be daunting. (Before tools like PartMaker, this sort of work was done by "summer interns." Today, we are fortunate to have such tools, since the summer interns are getting smarter about what constitutes drudgery and what constitutes valuable workplace experience.)

The code that follows is in fact output from PartMaker. As it did with the IDL file, PartMaker concatenates the part name and the author name to make (one can hope) unique identifiers. This practice is good, but it does tend to lead to some rather long variable names. Again, don't worry, because you will rarely see them. Also, ignore for the moment such keywords as SOM_Scope and SOMLINK. Further, ignore the code that is inserted for debugging purposes and that gets an object's data. Instead, look in each method for the line marked ⊃.

```
SOM_Scope void SOMLINK
som_DemoPart__somInit(PhilmontSoftware_som_DemoPart
*somSelf)

{
```

```
        PhilmontSoftware_som_DemoPartData *somThis =
PhilmontSoftware_som_DemoPartGetData(somSelf);

PhilmontSoftware_som_DemoPartMethodDebug("PhilmontSoft-
ware_som_DemoPart","som_DemoPart__somInit");


    // somInit and somUninit methods behave like C++
    // constructors in that the
    // inherited methods are called automatically.
    // Thus, there is no need to
    // call the parent class's somInit or somUninit.
    // *** This is unique to these methods.
    // You usually do call inherited somInit or
    // somUninit.
    // There is also no need to set instance variables
    // to zero/NULL
    // since SOM guarantees that a newly constructed
    // object is zeroed.


⊃   _fPart = new DemoPart;
}


SOM_Scope void SOMLINK
som_DemoPart__somUninit(PhilmontSoftware_som_DemoPart
*somSelf)
{
        PhilmontSoftware_som_DemoPartData *somThis =
PhilmontSoftware_som_DemoPartGetData(somSelf);

PhilmontSoftware_som_DemoPartMethodDebug("PhilmontSoft-
ware_som_DemoPart","som_DemoPart__somUninit");


⊃   delete _fPart;
}


SOM_Scope ODSize SOMLINK
```

```
som_DemoPart__Purge(PhilmontSoftware_som_DemoPart
*somSelf, Environment *ev,
        ODSize size)
{
    SOM_CATCH return 0;

    PhilmontSoftware_som_DemoPartData *somThis =
PhilmontSoftware_som_DemoPartGetData(somSelf);
    PhilmontSoftware_som_DemoPartMethodDebug("Philmont-
Software_som_DemoPart","som_DemoPart__Purge");

⊃    return _fPart->Purge(ev,size);
}


SOM_Scope void SOMLINK
som_DemoPart__Externalize(PhilmontSoftware_som_DemoPart
*somSelf, Environment *ev)
{
    SOM_CATCH return;

    PhilmontSoftware_som_DemoPartData *somThis =
PhilmontSoftware_som_DemoPartGetData(somSelf);

PhilmontSoftware_som_DemoPartMethodDebug("PhilmontSoft-
ware_som_DemoPart","som_DemoPart__Externalize");

    PhilmontSoftware_som_DemoPart_parent_ODPart_Exter-
nalize(somSelf,ev);

⊃    _fPart->Externalize(ev);
}
```

Note how the part is created and deleted when the SOMInit or SOMUninit methods are called. In the Externalize method, the part (in the variable _fPart) is asked to invoke its Externalize method.

This is the magic that links the SOM objects with your own objects. This is also the template for any additions you need to make to the generated code. To implement a method of a SOM class, you add its method declaration to the IDL file. Then modify the implementation file to add the method implementation with a call so as to pass control off to the actual object you are coding. As the previous code sample shows, there are some cases when you don't pass control to your code at all (new and delete calls). In other cases, you call a similarly named method in your own code, and in others, you call one of your own methods that accomplishes the task but is named something else.

Finally, for methods that do not need to be visible to the outside world through SOM (to other parts or OpenDoc itself, for example), you need not modify the IDL file at all.

The SOM Compiler

The SOM compiler takes your IDL file (which normally is produced by an automated tool) and generates header files for clients and implementors. In the integrated environments used for most OpenDoc development, all of these files will live together in a folder/directory call SOM or something similar. Sometimes they are inside an Includes folder/directory.

xh Files

A file with a .xh suffix is produced to be used as a header file for clients of your SOM objects (people who will use or subclass the part).

xih Files

The .xih file that is produced is used for the implementor of your object, someone who will need reference to the lines of code compiled with the conditional PRIVATE compiler directive.

The SOM Runtime Library

The last part of SOM you need to know about is its runtime library that actually links classes together. This is discussed in Chapter 9, "Putting It Together: OpenDoc at Runtime."

Summary

There are two important lessons in this chapter. First, SOM is an impressive solution to a thorny problem. It is complete, robust, and flexible, providing OpenDoc with a great deal of its power to combine parts and part editors on the fly.

Second, the power and complexity of SOM are largely hidden from you. Most of the writing of the SOM code is done automatically, either by OpenDoc tools like PartMaker or by the SOM compiler. What little code you do need to implement is straightforward and repetitive and consists largely of passing control to a method that you have written in your standard programming language and style.

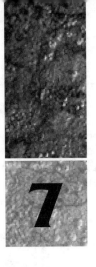

7

Managing OpenDoc Files and Storage: The Container Suite

Building on SOM, OpenDoc has a robust mechanism for combining objects at runtime, even if they are developed in various languages and are running on a network of different computers. Once these objects have been pulled together into a single Open-Doc document, they function as a well-integrated unit, fulfilling the wishes of the user.

All goes swimmingly until the user chooses the Save command. These objects that happily have been working together now will respond individually to this command—each one will write out its own data in its own format to disk. Obviously, this is a critical juncture at which chaos can rear its ugly head. Because OpenDoc is document-centric, users have the perfectly reasonable expectation that their OpenDoc document will live in a single file, no matter how many parts it contains. But a single file containing multiple formats and idiosyncratic data structures would be a nightmare. The OpenDoc designers designed a **container suite** API which defines a platform- and content-neutral storage specification for OpenDoc. **Bento** (which was created independently of OpenDoc—as was SOM) was designed to store and interchange multiple types of data in compound documents and is ideally suited to the data storage needs of OpenDoc. It is used to implement OpenDoc's container suite API.

In this chapter, you will find an overview of the OpenDoc container suite. As with SOM (and many other parts of OpenDoc), developers and designers rarely have to deal with the actual Bento API. The reading and writing routines from an ODF example part are annotated, showing the few Bento calls that a developer needs to worry about.

> Bento is the Japanese word for a box lunch as well as for a box or basket with compartments for different objects. This picturesque, evocative, and quite apt word tends not to be used in official OpenDoc documentation, which refers rather prosaically to the "OpenDoc Storage System." Unfortunately, this prosaic terminology has crept into the documentation and thrived. OpenDoc does not read and write data; it internalizes and externalizes it. This terminology represents one of the very few cases where OpenDoc actually complicates life rather than simplifying it. The use of the words "internalize" and "externalize" in this book should not be taken as an endorsement of this obfuscatory practice.

OpenDoc Storage Requirements

OpenDoc lets people put things together. Although a quintessentially human activity, it is one that rapidly gets incredibly complex. Often, the process of assembling an OpenDoc document involves a number of different people at a number of different locations, often running a number of different types of computers. The sequential access methods of simple document storage quickly become impractical in such an environment. At the other extreme, databases (including object oriented-databases) provide too much functionality for many relatively simple tasks. What OpenDoc requires for the bulk of its documents is a system that allows data to be stored and modified in a basically random—as opposed to sequential—manner. Such a system also would permit version information to be stored so that modifications can be rolled back or undone, even when they have been done at different times and by different people.

Bento

The OpenDoc container APIs is implemented using Bento. As a light-weight, powerful, cross-platform, commercially proven technology, it provides the functionality of the basic container suite for OpenDoc. (In addition to OpenDoc, Bento is used in Common Ground, Lotus 1-2-3 for Windows, and Avid OMFI.)

Storage Units and Their Properties

Bento is not a database. It is a simple way of storing a network of objects that are themselves very simple. These parts, called **storage units**, have a unique ID and a number of properties. Each property contains one piece of information, but it may contain multiple copies of this information in varying formats.

Each OpenDoc part has a primary storage unit that contains its data. A part may have auxiliary storage units to store additional data in a manner that is up to the designer and developer. However, one of those storage units must be primary.

Figure 7-1 shows a schematic representation of a storage unit, its properties, and their values.

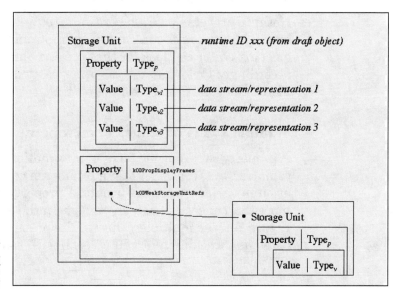

Figure 7-1.

A storage unit, its properties, and their values

Standard Properties

For OpenDoc parts to be combined and to work together, certain standard OpenDoc properties and types are used repeatedly. This allows part editors to query and manipulate the properties of parts created by other part editors.

For example, a standard property type of OpenDoc parts is identified by the constant kODPropDraftComments. In the schematic shown in Figure 7-1, the property's identifier is shown as its type, $Type_p$. This property contains comments about the draft. It might contain a number of values of differing types. One value might be of type TEXT and consist of the phrase, "This part reflects Joe's comments from Monday." Another value for that same property might be of type RTF, and consist of the phrase, "This part reflects *Joe's* comments from *Monday*." Any part editor can look for the kODPropDraftComments property of any storage unit, and, if it finds it, can then look for a type of value that it can display.

Developers and designers will do well to study the list of standard OpenDoc properties in the OpenDoc Class Reference. To achieve maximum flexibility and reuse of parts, you should use the standard properties wherever possible. Furthermore, the more specific the property, the better.

Nothing prevents a developer from creating a property identified by the idiosyncratic constant kMyPropComments. That developer's part editor can look for that property and handle its data accordingly. Unfortunately, no other part editor will find the comments relevant to that storage unit.

Multiple Types of Values in a Property

A property contains one piece of information (which may be very complex), but it may contain a number of copies of that information in various types or formats. A property can never contain more than one value of a given type. In the schematic shown in Figure 7-1, the multiple values of the property of type $Type_p$ are listed as three different values, each with a type $Type_{v1}$, $Type_{v2}$, or $Type_{v3}$.

For example, the developer could store a date as a TEXT string, an RTF string, a platform-specific date, and as a timestamp in a format that is unique to a specific organization (e.g., "in the fifth year of the reign of King Harold"). Part editors that want to access the property may select the format that is most appropriate for their use.

Types as Streams

A value can be a complex structure, possibly of very large size. OpenDoc storage allows you to treat the type as a stream, which means you can read and write to it sequentially as well as insert, modify, and delete data at specific locations within the value. The container suite is sophisticated and efficient about performing these operations with a minimum of system resources.

Types as References

In addition to storing simple and complex data types, you will frequently need to store references to other objects in a storage unit. For example, a standard property type is kODPropDisplayFrames, a list of a part's display frames (each of which is stored in its own storage unit).

Storage units are uniquely identified by the container suite, but you never directly manipulate the identifier. If you want to store the list of display frames for a part, you ask its storage unit for a reference for the frame's storage unit, and you then store that reference in the kODPropDisplayFrames property of the part's storage unit. In the schematic shown in Figure 7-1, the unique reference identifier is shown with a black dot to signify the fact that you don't manipulate it directly.

You may question the quick method of getting the list of a part's display frames. Remember that frames are types of ODPersistentObject and that there are only two ways to initialize these objects:

```
void InitPersistentObject (
    in ODStorageUnit storageUnit);
```

```
void InitPersistentObjectFromStorage(
    in ODStorageUnit storageUnit);
```

Every persistent object has a storage unit associated with it.

You frequently do refer to storage units at runtime by using the transient identifier that is supplied to you when you create a storage unit. (You can create or acquire a storage unit. An acquired storage unit is one that has been created previously and is now being reinstantiated.) The transient identifiers assigned at runtime are unique within a draft of a document, but they are not permanently unique and should never be stored.

Using Storage Units

The only things stored inside a storage unit are values and properties and their associated types. (Storage units and properties use the Bento mechanism and collapse to the same structure. A storage unit consists of a storage unit identifying type; its value is a reference to an object that is a list of its properties. Each property consists of a property type. The value of the type is a reference to an object that is a list of the ultimate property value/type combinations.)

Focusing on Storage Unit Locations

Because it is so important for the container suite to support random access to information, focus routines are provided to point you quickly to the appropriate part of a storage unit. There are four ways to focus:

1. *Property/value names.* As each property/value type combination must be unique within a storage unit, you can focus on a property/value directly.

2. *Property name/value order.* You can focus on the *n*th value for a given property. This makes it easy to iterate through all of a property's values.

3. *Next/previous property/value.* These methods make it easy to iterate through all properties and/or all values of a storage unit.

4. *Cursors.* Once you have found a location in a storage unit, you can create a cursor that points to that location and return to it by focusing on that cursor.

Once you have obtained a focus on a location within a storage unit, you may refocus using any of the relative positioning constructs shown in Table 7-1.

Table 7-1.

Focusing on a storage unit location using relative positions

Property type	Value type
Property type	*n*th value (starting from 1)
Current property	next/previous property
Current property	current value next/previous value
Cursor*	

*A cursor can be initialized with a storage unit focus that is normally obtained by using one of the other focus methods and then stored for reuse.

Writing to Storage Units

To write information to a storage unit, you need only position yourself to the appropriate property/value location. Where new data is being written out, the steps are as follows:

1. Add the property to the given storage unit ("su" in this example).

```
su->AddProperty (ev, kTheProperty);
```

2. Add the type for the value to be written.

```
su->AddValue (ev, kValueType);
```

3. Position the container to this location.

```
su->Focus (ev, kTheProperty, kValueType);
    //this is a simplified version of the
    //actual call
```

4. Locate the starting position within the data stream of the value.

```
su->SetOffset (ev, thePosition);
```

5. Set the value.

```
su->SetValue (ev, byteArray);
```

The OpenDoc structure ODByteArray wraps data types larger than 4 bytes. Its fields include the data buffer, its size, and the maximum size the buffer might ever reach.

In actual practice, this code is usually modified; the properties and values are added only if they don't already exist.

The process of reading from storage units is comparable to writing.

Documents and Drafts

Storage units—one or more for each persistent object in an OpenDoc document—are combined into documents. The OpenDoc container suite manages documents and usually stores each document as an individual file on disk or in memory.

Because a document consists of a group of storage units, and OpenDoc does not rely on sequential processes to store its data, it is not difficult to support multiple drafts of documents. This is an important aspect of OpenDoc. Remember that one of the ways of combining tools, ideas, and information is in an experimental manner. Experiments are far more willingly undertaken if they are reversible.

OpenDoc allows only one user to edit a document's draft at a time and only the most recent draft of a document can be edited at all. It is up to the OpenDoc user to decide when a new draft should be started. Where there are many users, each working on a single machine, their documents often will have only one draft. In the case of far-flung workgroups, drafts are used more frequently.

The OpenDoc Draft History dialog box allows users to inspect the draft status of their documents. For each draft, the creator and timestamp are shown. (There is only one creator of a draft, since only one person can work on a draft at a single time. Once the draft has been created, other users may work on it, provided they have the appropriate permissions enforced by OpenDoc and the operating system.) In addition, a brief comment about the draft (such as, "final version—we hope" or "initial draft") is shown.

Drafts can be deleted when they are no longer necessary in order to clean up storage. Also, although only the most recent draft can be edited, previous drafts can still be opened and material copied out of them, in case, say, last Thursday's bad idea suddenly looks good on Monday.

Containers

The OpenDoc storage mechanism consists of storage units that are aggregated into drafts that in turn live within documents. In its design, OpenDoc has two higher levels in its storage mechanism. The basic OpenDoc storage system manages the implementation of storage. OpenDoc allows many different storage technologies to be used, such as file systems and object-oriented databases. Each of these is implemented as a container suite in accordance with the OpenDoc container API.

Currently, a cross-platform container suite implemented using Bento is used by OpenDoc.

OpenDoc Storage: An Example

The Text Editor example on the OpenDoc SDK demonstrates the use of Bento. Annotated excerpts from that example follow. These routines are used in writing out the Text Editor part; reading is similar.

One of the methods of ODPersistentObject that must be overridden is the Externalize method, which is responsible for moving the part's data out to the storage system:

```
void
SOMLINK      TextEditor__Externalize(
    SampleCode_TextEditor*      somSelf,
    Environment*                ev)
{
    // This is boilerplate SOM code
    SampleCode_TextEditorData *somThis =
        SampleCode_TextEditorGetData
        (somSelf);

    SOM_CATCH return;
```

```
// First, ask our parent classes to
// externalize themselves.
parent_Externalize(somSelf, ev);

// Only write the part out if it's
// changed. Note that the
// parent classes are given the
// chance to write themselves out
// even if we are not dirty.
if (_fDirty)
{
    // Get our storage unit.
    ODStorageUnit* storageUnit =
        somSelf->GetStorageUnit(ev);

    // Verify that the storage unit has
    // the appropriate properties
    // and values to allow us to run
    // If not, add them.
    // (See code below.)
    somSelf->CheckAndAddProperties(
        ev, storageUnit);

    // Verify that there are no "bogus"
    // values in the Content property.
    // (See code below.)
    somSelf->CleanseContentProperty(
        ev, storageUnit);

    // Write out the part's state
    // information.
    // (See code below.)
    somSelf->ExternalizeStateInfo(
        ev, storageUnit, 0, kODNULL);
```

```
        // Write out the part's content.
        // (See code below.)
        somSelf->ExternalizeContent(
            ev, storageUnit, kODNULL);

        _fDirty = kODFalse;

    }

}
```

This routine, called from Externalize, checks whether specific
properties exist in the storage unit; if not, they are added. On
completion, all of this part's properties will be present in the
storage unit.

```
void
SOMLINK       TextEditor__CheckAndAddProperties(
    SampleCode_TextEditor*        somSelf,
    Environment*                  ev,
    ODStorageUnit*                storageUnit)
{

    // This is boilerplate SOM code
    SampleCode_TextEditorData *somThis =
        SampleCode_TextEditorGetData
        (somSelf);

    // Create our content property.
    // In reality, there is an "else"
    // for this if to update existing
    // properties and their values.
    if ( !storageUnit->Exists(
        ev,
        kODPropContents, //standard
                      //property type for
                      //contents of a
                      //part
```

```
        kODNULL,
        0) )
        storageUnit->AddProperty(
            ev, kODPropContents);
// Create the property value
if ( !storageUnit->Exists(
        ev,
        kODPropContents,
        kTextEditorKind, //the data in
                    // this property is
                    // text editing
                    // data
        0) )
        {
        storageUnit->Focus(
            ev,
            kODPropContents,
            kODPosUndefined,
            kODNULL,
            0,
            kODPosUndefined);
        storageUnit->AddValue(
            ev, kTextEditorKind);
        }
// Add another value for this
// property (scrap text)
if ( !storageUnit->Exists(
        ev,
        kODPropContents,
        gScrapTextValue,
        0) )
        {
```

```
            storageUnit->Focus(
                ev,
                kODPropContents,
                kODPosUndefined,
                kODNULL,
                0,
                kODPosUndefined);
            storageUnit->AddValue(ev,
                gScrapTextValue);
            }
    }

    // Add our display frame list.
    if (!storageUnit->Exists(
        ev,
        kODPropDisplayFrames,
        kODNULL,
        0))
        storageUnit->AddProperty(ev,
            kODPropDisplayFrames);

}
void
SOMLINK        TextEditor__CleanseContentProperty(
    SampleCode_TextEditor*        somSelf,
    Environment*                  ev,
    ODStorageUnit*                storageUnit)
{
    SampleCode_TextEditorData *somThis =
        SampleCode_TextEditorGetData
        (somSelf);
    SOMMethodDebug(
        "TextEditor","Externalize");
```

```
SOM_CATCH return;

ODULong numValues;
ODULong index;

storageUnit->Focus(
    ev, kODPropContents,
    kODPosUndefined,
    kODNULL, 0, kODPosAll);

numValues = storageUnit->CountValues(ev);

for (index = numValues;
    index > 0;
    index--)
{
    // Index from n to 1
    // through the values.
    storageUnit->Focus(
        ev, kODPropContents,
        kODPosUndefined,

        kODNULL, index,
        kODPosUndefined);
    ODValueType value =
        storageUnit->GetType(ev);

    // If the value type is not
    // one we support, remove it.
    if ( (ODISOStrCompare(value,
        kTextEditorKind) != 0) &&
        (ODISOStrCompare(value,
        gScrapTextValue) != 0) )
        storageUnit->Remove(ev);
```

```
            ODDisposePtr(value);

    }

}
void
SOMLINK      TextEditor__ExternalizeContent
        (
        SampleCode_TextEditor* somSelf,
        Environment*           ev,
        ODStorageUnit*         storageUnit,
        ODPtr                  selRange
        )
{
  SampleCode_TextEditorData *somThis =
        SampleCode_TextEditorGetData
        (somSelf);
  SOMMethodDebug(
        "TextEditor","ExternalizeContent");

   ❶if (_fTextensionInitialized)
    {
        ODSLong start, end;

        // If there is a "open" inline
        // hole, we need to close it
        // before saving.
        if ( _fTextension
            >HasActiveInputArea(
           &start, &end) )
           _fTextension->
               FixActiveInputArea();
        // Write out native Textension
        // data format
```

```
storageUnit->Focus(
        ev, kODPropContents,
        kODPosUndefined,
        kTextEditorKind, 0,
        kODPosUndefined);

somSelf->StreamDataOut(
        ev, storageUnit->CreateView
        (ev), selRange, kIOAll);

// Write out plain text for
// compatibility with other parts

if ( storageUnit->Exists(
        ev, kODPropContents,
        gScrapTextValue, 0) )
{
        storageUnit->Focus(
                ev, kODPropContents,
                kODPosUndefined,
                gScrapTextValue, 0,
                kODPosUndefined);

        somSelf->StreamDataOut(
                ev,
                storageUnit->CreateView
                        (ev),
                selRange, kNoIOFlags);
}
    ❷}
}
```

Note that the code between ❶ and ❷ is specific to this example. The structure of this method applies to all parts; each one will have a very different implementation of this section.

Summary

OpenDoc's storage services are an abstraction that provides for platform- and content-neutral data storage. Implemented with Bento, the storage mechanism supports multiple drafts of documents and optimizes the frequent, relatively small changes made to compound documents.

This chapter summarizes the features of OpenDoc's storage and describes some of the more common routines. For most developers, their use of the storage routines will be relatively unthinking. This is boilerplate code that is copied from one part editor to another, and—in the case of development frameworks—is largely hidden.

As a designer or developer, you can rely on OpenDoc's robustness and flexibility when it comes to data storage. Remember to check the list of standard OpenDoc property and value types before creating your own. Using standard types will make it easier for other parts to inspect and use your data. Opening your part and its data up to the world increases its value.

When you use the standard property and value types, people can see what you've got in your part (although how you do it remains proprietary and hidden in your source code). It would certainly increase the value of your part if people could see in a standard way exactly what you can do—and even ask you to do it. What a wonderful idea! What a great increase in value to users! Why didn't they think of that!

They did. It's called OSA, and it's described in the next chapter.

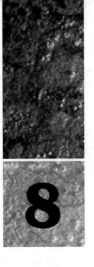

8

Managing OpenDoc Communications: OSA

OpenDoc is about putting ideas, tools, and information together in almost any way you want, ideally without regard to the software, operating systems, or networks involved. OpenDoc manages the basic interaction and communication among parts in a compound document, making certain they properly divide up the available space on the screen or page as well as ensuring they properly divide up keyboard, mouse, and menu events.

Some interactions must be more specific and customized to the contents and capabilities of individual parts. A spell-checking part may well have a thing or two to say to various text parts in a document, and a number of mechanisms are provided that allow this communication to take place.

Beyond the needs of the parts in one (or more) OpenDoc documents, the issue of scripting arises when users want to have alternative means of controlling their computers. For all the work that has gone into developing ergonomic keyboards, intuitive menus, and the other features of a sophisticated user experience, sometimes the user has a better idea. In fact, often it is only as users start to combine tools in new ways that interfaces "break." (One classic example is the user who found a way to use Microsoft Excel —a spreadsheet application—to host a multimedia presentation with QuickTime movies. It worked very well, although the standard Excel command bar did look a little strange.)

In this chapter is an overview of scripting in general and the Open Scripting Architecture (OSA) that OpenDoc uses. Following that is a discussion of OpenDoc's scripting implementation.

Scripting is important to all aspects of OpenDoc. If you are developing or designing OpenDoc parts, you should include some level of support for scripting. If you are assembling a solution out of existing or custom-written OpenDoc parts, scripting may be the way to tie things together. Finally, if you are integrating OpenDoc with existing applications, using OSA may make your life easier.

Scripting and the Open Scripting Architecture

One problem with putting things together in the computer world is getting the interfaces to work properly. Different applications (even within the same general area of functionality) have different terminologies. An advantage of a graphical user interface—the ability to directly manipulate the program and its elements—is a disadvantage when you are combining applications and you just want application X to do one thing and then go away.

People found the need to automate computer applications very early. Batch-oriented processes, run from commands stored on punched cards or in disk files, were easy to automate. Many an old program punched out a new deck of cards to be used as input to itself or another application later on.

Batch files in the DOS world provided a similar capability on a limited scale: Applications could be started, and basic DOS commands could be stored in a file. Applications could generate and modify these batch files, and many did so. However, the problems of inconsistent terminologies among applications limited the usefulness of these batch files.

In the world of graphical user interfaces, scripting began to be implemented when keystrokes and mouse clickings could be stored in a file for future use. These files were (and are!) very popular and automated many tasks.

One of the biggest drawbacks with such batch files, however, is that they are simply a list of commands to be sent to the computer. They provide little feedback from either the user, the operating system, or the application programs. Thus arises the frustratingly common case where the logon to a computer host requires one additional entry (and one additional carriage return) since the batch file was prepared. You can watch in horror as the file continues past the point with the changed prompt and all of its commands are sent off into Neverland.

As conditional statements (If/Then/Else) and control statements (While/For loops) were added to try to ameliorate these problems and to further enhance the power of batch files, those files began to evolve into something resembling a primitive computer language. Unfortunately, these batch files remain highly unstable and sensitive to the least little change in any interface.

Semantic Interfaces

OSA was devised to address the issue of scripting—that is, indirect or batch manipulation of applications—from a new point of view. Instead of its trying to mimic keystrokes and mouse clicks, OSA is built on a *semantic* basis: Its commands and instructions address the meaningful functionalities of a program.

For example, to change a word to boldface type, you select the word (either by double-clicking it or by dragging along it with the mouse) and then choose Bold from the appropriate menu. To automate this process in interface-oriented automation systems, you must somehow determine the position of the word so as to simulate the mouse click or double-click and then issue the command to choose Bold from the menu. Here is an example of the problem with such systems: If the window is scrolled slightly, the word's location may change and the wrong word may be selected by the script.

In OSA's semantic interface, you issue a command along the lines of "set the style of word 2 of paragraph 1 to bold." You address the meaningful action, not the physical interface commands that cause that action. These are not isolated commands and instructions: they are **semantic events**. Semantic events are usually those things that someone who doesn't know how to use the program would know how to say.

OSA Components

OSA is implemented with three components: an event messaging system, an object model, and a scripting system. It should be noted that OSA was first implemented on the Mac OS with Apple events and AppleScript. Today, this represents its fullest implementation. With the advent of OpenDoc, however, OSA will be used more on other platforms. Because the Mac OS implementation is currently the fullest, this chapter presents code on that platform. In general, identifiers and methods starting with the letters OD are implemented by OpenDoc and are cross-platform. Identifiers and methods starting with AE (for Apple events) are specific to the Mac OS. Comparable identifiers and methods for the other platforms will be provided with the final platform implementations of OpenDoc for those platforms. The functionality (not the means of accomplishing it) will be comparable to that on the Mac OS.

Because OSA deals with information on a higher, more abstract level than that of keystrokes, it needs more sophisticated data structures and control mechanisms. These are provided in its events, its object model, and the scripting systems that support it.

> This section describes OSA in its basic form. Some modifications are made in its implementation with OpenDoc; these are discussed in the next section. Here the basic OSA architecture in the context of traditional applications is detailed.

Events

Messages are sent to applications to instruct them what actions to take as part of OSA. In this way, OSA is not so different from other macro and automated processes. However, OSA goes far beyond these processes by allowing messages to be sent from applications, either in response to an initial message or for other reasons.

The messages—which are called **events**—are highly structured in a number of ways. In the first, their internal structure consists of an action (the event), as well as an optional direct object on which the action is performed. In addition, a number of parameters may be provided that are specific to the event. The application that receives the event uses standard routines to extract the direct object (if it exists) and the parameters (if they exist). OSA defines many standard data types that can be sent in these events. Users can provide additional types if they are necessary.

In the second way, events are grouped into suites. Each event is uniquely identified by a suite identifier and its event identifier. Suites have been defined for basic functionality (a core suite), as well as for domain-specific uses (a text editing suite, a database suite, and so on). Developers are encouraged to use and reuse these events wherever possible. This makes it easier for users to script different applications that share common functionalities.

If a standard event suite is not available, developers can create new ones. If an existing suite is available, developers are able to extend it if additional functionality is required. The sharing of events and suites of events does not compromise the integrity and uniqueness of an individual application. Applications are differentiated by the combinations of events they can perform and the speed and ease with which they do so.

Object Model

Within the structure of events, parameters of events can be used to specify objects on which to operate as well as parameters to be applied to those objects. The taxonomic structure of these objects and their properties is called the **object model**. Once again, the basic suites (described in *Apple Event Registry Standard Suites*) provide the basics for the object model. OSA implements an efficient means of parsing syntax that describes objects by their ordinal positions within containers (e.g., the third word of paragraph 2), but the designer must choose what the objects are and what their containment hierarchy should be.

Fortunately, between the standards developed for OSA and the commonsense observations of people who are familiar with the information a particular application deals with, developing an object model is usually not a particularly onerous task for the designer. Once the object model has been designed, it is up to the developer to implement the code that will allow OSA to find the nth thing in the mth container. But that code is normally routine and boilerplate. Development frameworks particularly on the Mac OS provide this support routinely.

Scripting Systems

The final component of OSA is the scripting system that is used to generate scripts and to run them on a specific platform. Userland Frontier and AppleScript are two fully configured scripting systems for the Mac OS. Any OSA-compliant scripting system will work with OpenDoc. Other scripting systems, some incorporating sophisticated graphical interfaces to their scripts, are bound to appear on all platforms that support OpenDoc.

OpenDoc's Scripting Implementation

OpenDoc's scripting implementation is based on OSA. Certain modifications are needed so that the application-centric world in which OSA was developed maps appropriately and easily onto OpenDoc's world.

OpenDoc technical documentation provides descriptions of how OpenDoc manages events and how it resolves references to objects within parts (the second paragraph of part "anni," for example). Above that fine level of detail, three important elements of OpenDoc's scripting implementation are discussed here: levels of scriptability, the semantic interface, and the message interface.

Levels of Scriptability

From the beginning, OSA has supported the notion of different levels of scriptability. In OpenDoc, there are four. The first three are progressively more sophisticated and complex.

An OpenDoc part may be

1. scriptable,
2. customizable, and/or
3. tinkerable.

Each of these levels builds on the previous one. In addition, there is a fourth level of scriptability that may be implemented with any (or none) of the above levels. That is, an OpenDoc part may be recordable.

Scriptable

The most basic level, that of scriptability, allows the basic objects and operations of a part to be visible from the outside and for these to be accessible by events. In most cases, these objects and operations are visible to the human eye and hand. Making your part scriptable requires that these objects and operations be described in a terminology resource that can be read by a scripting system and displayed for the script writer.

Remember that at the most basic level, your content objects and operations should relate more to the task or activity that the user is doing than to the particular implementation, internal data structures, or programming logic you are providing. In other words, it is generally far more important for the scriptwriter to be able to apply boldface style to the second word of the third paragraph than to be able to select the second item in the third menu. The first case is related to the activity; the second is related to the computer.

At a more complete level, your objects may include your interface elements. However, basic scriptability requires only that the substance of your part be exposed to the outside world.

Customizable

To make your part customizable, you must make the interface elements of your part (buttons, menus, palettes) visible. In addition, your part must provide the ability to store any scripts that may have been attached by a user to these interface elements. By attaching scripts to interface elements, users can modify the behavior of these elements, usually by extending and enhancing their basic features.

As with the use of overloaded functions and operators in C++, the creative/devious scriptwriter can wreak havoc with this feature. It's a barely amusing parlor game to change the action of the Bold button to italicize text. For that reason, you may want to enforce the convention that a customized script attached to an interface element cannot replace certain basic functionality. With such a notion, you would always have, at a minimum, a Bold button actually boldface the current selection.

But wait. In some fonts and in some environments, boldfacing is not appropriate. Maybe the user legitimately wants to add the emphasis of boldface by changing the color of the type to red. In such a case, maybe you would not want to have a minimum functionality enforced. Is there no clearcut answer? Do you suddenly feel like Alice, surrounded by queens, white rabbits, and mad hatters?

Relax and look at things in perspective. The user (as always) is interested in a task or activity. The means to the end are relatively unimportant. The user most likely doesn't care whether selected text is boldfaced; the user simply wants to emphasize a section of text. If you go back to the simplest, most basic view of things, you can see that providing a level of abstraction that makes sense to the user often will clean up your interface. Perhaps you want an Emphasize button. If your part is customizable, that button may use boldface, color, or even changes in pitch and volume (for spoken text) to achieve the goal. Remember that with OpenDoc, you are finally able to focus on where you should: on people and their activities.

Tinkerable

A tinkerable part is totally scriptable and customizable; every action that the part may undertake may be scripted, and those scripts must be stored with the part. This means not only that the part's own interface elements are scriptable, but also that actions that are controlled by the root or containing part or even OpenDoc itself (open, save, close, and so on) must be scriptable.

Recordable

The final level of scriptability is to make a part recordable. Recordability may be coupled with any, all, or none of the other three levels of scriptability. If you separate your part's content model from its interface, you may well implement the part's functionality by sending events from your interface elements to your part. There is a simplicity in this. It allows your part to do its work in response to events that may be generated by your interface or equally may be generated by events coming from other parts or from a user-written script.

Such a structure (which is becoming more common even in traditional applications) easily allows for recordability of scripts. As each event is received, it can be stored and then written out for future use. Users find recordable parts immensely helpful. Instead of the user's studying even a simple description of a part's objects and operations, the user does something close to what is desired, inspects the recorded script, and manually makes any changes necessary.

At a minimum, your parts should provide basic scriptability and recordability. These two features enhance and extend the ability of OpenDoc parts to be joined together in interesting and adventuresome ways.

Semantic Interface

OpenDoc extensions were discussed in Chapter 5. Basically, any descendant of ODObject can have an extension that can be found and used at runtime. OpenDoc's implementation of OSA uses Semantic Extension objects, which are descendants of ODExtension. By using the ODObject routines HasExtension and AcquireExtension, any OpenDoc Object (including any part, root part, or the OpenDoc shell itself), can determine if your part has its own semantic interface.

Accessing a Part's Semantic Interface

The following code from the HelloPart sample demonstrates this:

```
ODBoolean CPHelloPart::HasExtension(
    Environment* ev, ODType extensionName)
```

```
{
    if (!ODISOStrCompare(
            (ODISOStr)extensionName,
            kODExtSemanticInterface))
        return kODTrue;
    else
        return kODFalse;
}
```

Anyone who wants to inquire if your part supports a semantic interface extension can call this routine with this line:

```
if yourPart->HasExtension (
    ev, kODExtSemanticInterface)
```

Obviously, if you pass in kODExtSemanticInterface in the extensionName parameter it will match the constant in the If statement, and kODTrue will be returned. (Remember that ODISOStr-Compare, like C string utilities, can return three values based on the comparison. A value of 0 means the two strings are equal; 0 also is the Boolean false, which is why the code is written as it is.)

Similarly, any OpenDoc element that wants to access your semantic interface can use the AcquireExtension method (which you will have overridden) to get your semantic interface. In actual practice, it is most often OpenDoc itself that will be getting your semantic interface, not other parts (except in fairly sophisticated interpart solutions).

Writing a Semantic Interface

You must write a semantic interface (a descendant of ODSemanticInterface) that is specific to your part. The methods of ODSemanticInterface are primarily of two types:

1. Semantic Handlers process the events sent to your semantic interface (think of these as verb-handlers).

2. Object-Accessor Handlers access and resolve references to objects in your part's content model (think of these as noun-handlers).

There are several ways to create semantic interfaces for your parts. You can subclass ODSemanticInterface directly. OpenDoc also provides another development structure in which the utility class CplusSemanticInterface can be used together with a subclass of the much smaller SIHelperAbs class. Further, OpenDoc provides a default semantic interface for all parts that provides basic functionality. Finally, development environments such as ODF provide basic implementations of semantic interfaces for you to build on.

Message Interface

Semantic interfaces allow a part to receive, process, and often reply to an incoming event. A **message interface** allows a part to send an event on its own, not merely a reply to an incoming event.

You can send events to anything that is capable of receiving them: your own part, other parts, even traditional applications. Designing your part so that it sends events to itself makes it recordable with very little effort.

Message interfaces are implemented in the class ODMessageInterface. Routines in ODMessageInterface let you create events, place data in them, and then send them off to the appropriate destination. One ODMessageInterface object is shared by all parts; the ODSession routine GetMessageInterface returns this shared object:

```
ODMessageInterface GetMessageInterface ();
```

Summary

OpenDoc's scripting capabilities are an important way in which it delivers the ability to combine parts in ways that matter to users. Providing minimal scripting for your parts (basic scriptability and recordability) helps users incorporate those parts in automated solutions. The semantic-based OSA technology provides a high-level, cross-platform, meaningful way of automating and combining processes on one or more computers. It is a far cry from the keystroke macros and batch files of the past. Furthermore, it can allow a bridge between OpenDoc parts and traditional applications, provided the parts and the traditional application support at least minimal scriptability.

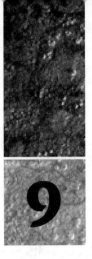

9

Putting It Together: OpenDoc at Runtime

The technical overview of OpenDoc concludes with this chapter, aptly enough returning to the theme presented in the Introduction and Chapter 1—putting it together. The behaviorial issues of putting ideas, information, and tools together were covered in Part I. In this part of the book, the OpenDoc technologies have been described generally:

- The basics of all OpenDoc parts (Chapter 5)
- OpenDoc's management of objects within a single address space on one machine or across multiple address spaces on various machines on several networks (SOM—Chapter 6)
- The way in which OpenDoc stores data (Chapter 7)
- OpenDoc's communications and automation features (OSA—Chapter 8).

Putting all of these together at runtime requires a few additional chores, and they are described in this chapter.

The goal of OpenDoc's runtime architecture is simple: Documents should behave as users expect them to, regardless of the computer, network, platform, or other environmental factors that may to be present. The runtime OpenDoc features of most importance to the designer and developer are OpenDoc's error control strategy, its management of resources (focusing and foci), its handling of drawing (facets), its treatment of data transfer and integration (cut/copy/paste and drag and drop), and most important of all, its actual integration of the necessary software so that a compound document functions as a seamless unit at runtime.

Unstoppable Software

Software isn't worth much if it doesn't run. OpenDoc is designed to be as unstoppable as possible.

It is remarkable how many things can stop software from running—and how much people are willing to put up with in this area! Missing fonts cause strange pagination in documents as they are moved from machine to machine. Limits of memory and disk space stop applications dead in their tracks more often than not. Upgrades to system software and applications frequently incorporate changes to file formats—once again freezing applications like a deer in a car's headlights. And of course, the biggest "stopper" of all is the fact that software and file formats are often incompatible across operating systems and even among different versions and varieties of what one would consider to be a "single" operating system.

There are several ways to increase the stability of software, particularly software as complex as OpenDoc, where components may be written by many different people and combined in unpredictable ways. One approach that has been taken is the complete closed design that was described in the Introduction. This is particularly so in a component design that is in widespread use and provides a small portion of OpenDoc's functionality. The rules are spelled out quite rigidly, and all players are expected to abide by them, neither modifying nor expanding them. This approach can appear at first glance to provide a more robust system than the open design of OpenDoc does. Unfortunately, the limitations of a complete closed design quickly surface in the software industry as boundaries are pushed and inconsistencies quickly flourish.

OpenDoc accepts the turmoil of the open design and is designed at every turn to deal with the consequences.

Ounces of Prevention and Pounds of Cure— OpenDoc's Error Control Strategy

A component-based software architecture is probably more prey to potential problems than are other types of software (although the massive benefits of component software far outweigh this disadvantage). Still, it is necessary to be prepared for the worst.

OpenDoc developers are constantly reminded that their software should be written in the simplest way possible. Throughout OpenDoc and ODF, error-checking routines abound and exception-handling code is built into all aspects of OpenDoc. A particularly nasty aspect of monster applications is that in their complexity, error-handling can get lost. Resizing a window after you have undone a font size change should not cause an application to crash. Because OpenDoc parts are much smaller and simpler, they should be able to trap their own errors more consistently, thereby preventing the problems that many users have encountered with monster applications.

Of course, the availability of error-checking and exception-handling routines is no guarantee that programmers will use them. Whether ruled by arrogance or self-assurance, some people find it hard to imagine that their code may fail—or that people will not behave precisely as they expect them to. OpenDoc certainly provides more support for managing unforeseen circumstances than do most systems and architectures, so it is safe to say that part editors simply should not crash or quit unexpectedly. Unfortunately, it is also true that people should not lie, cheat, or steal. The existence of goals and standards does not ensure they will be met.

The error control strategy in OpenDoc consists of proactive and reactive features. When properly used, OpenDoc and part editors should rarely cause catastrophic (or even noticeable) problems for the user. The errors, warnings, and alerts that are presented should (ideally) all be direct consequences of user actions, not of software anomalies.

Proactive Error Control

The most basic principle of OpenDoc's error control strategy is the assumption that everything can fail. Much of this support is integrated into OpenDoc and is not dependent on a part editor for its implementation. Three aspects of OpenDoc's proactive error control are discussed in this section: the ability to work around missing part editors, handling of low-memory situations, and the importance of simplicity.

Part Editors May Be Missing

OpenDoc provides default behavior for everything that an OpenDoc part must do in order to function minimally in a compound document. It provides a sophisticated system for locating an appropriate part editor, but if one cannot be found, OpenDoc can "cover" for it. All that is needed for minimal functionality is the ability to read and write the part and to display it. Without a part editor, OpenDoc can survive.

The storage system stores properties and values without regard to their internal formats. Thus OpenDoc can read and write a part's data by passing values and properties to and from a container suite without knowing what these items mean. (OpenDoc can even display the list of properties of a part without knowing what those properties might be.) Because the part's custom data is within storage unit values, parts can be manipulated and moved among documents—with their data—without a part editor's being present. (Of course, at some point a part editor will be needed to interpret the data from within the storage unit values.)

Furthermore, remember that it is the containing part (or root part) that ultimately determines a part's location and shape (although the part enters into negotiation with its container to determine these values). Because it is the containing part that is responsible for placing a part appropriately, OpenDoc can easily use the information in the frame of a containing part to draw a gray shape in the appropriate location and shape to represent a part that cannot draw itself.

Memory May Be Lacking

Another form of proactive error control is to prepare for low memory conditions. The Purge method belongs to the ODObject class. OpenDoc may ask any ODObject to relinquish memory at any time. Buffers, off-screen bitmaps, and scratch arrays are all candidates for purging. Unlike OpenDoc's mechanism for dealing with missing part editors, this does require implementation by the developer. Still, since OpenDoc itself provides the routines that decide when and how to free up memory, the difficulty of implementing a system to manage memory properly is greatly reduced.

Simplicity Is Actively Encouraged

The final component of OpenDoc's error control strategy is simplicity. Part editors are much smaller than applications. The complexity of code grows at least exponentially with its length. A routine that is one page long can be "tested" and "debugged" by being read by an experienced programmer. An application of several hundred thousand lines requires much more complicated procedures.

Although OpenDoc does not require developers to use object-oriented languages, most will. Object-oriented code itself is simpler than procedural code. The things that complicate traditional code tend to be absent in object-oriented programs. (Structured programming removed the "goto" statements from code; object-oriented programming removes many of the "if" and "case" statements that generate multiple paths through code.)

To fully use OpenDoc's proactive error control strategy, developers should make certain to implement the Purge method of every OpenDoc part that has *any* data members. Designers, for their part, should remember that simplicity pays and should keep part editors as lean as possible.

Reactive Error Control

OpenDoc's reactive error control strategy is implemented largely with the SOM environment parameter that is passed to all SOM objects. It is further implemented (in the C++ environment) with the catching and throwing of errors. These are both technical issues that are not specific to OpenDoc, and they are covered in programming references.

What is specific to OpenDoc is the red light that should flash in every designer's mind that says "this might not happen." It is simply not acceptable to throw up your programmatic hands when something untoward happens. Remember that OpenDoc can cover for you even if there is no part editor. Building on top of OpenDoc, the part editor developer has little to do other than implement part-specific functionality. But you should remember all of Open-Doc's support for failure and do your bit, chiefly by implementing the proactive schemes discussed earlier in the chapter.

Resource Management—Focusing and Foci

The operating system typically manages computer resources; it determines which process should get a mouse click or keystroke. The application itself then determines which of its windows gets the event. In OpenDoc, resources need to be managed down to a lower level; each part may need to have control of the menu bar, the keyboard, or other resources. This is accomplished with **foci**. A part can obtain the focus on the keyboard, and while it retains that focus, no other part can use the keyboard. OpenDoc provides an arbitrator to handle requests for foci from individual parts.

Developers and designers must remember to request—and relinquish—foci as needed. If they do so, they don't have to worry about handling extraneous events or about not having the system resources they need. The focusing system is designed to be extensible (as is all of OpenDoc). This means that resources that are not envisioned today (the smell sensor, for example) can be incorporated into OpenDoc tomorrow with minimal changes.

The arbitrator is sophisticated in its management of focus requests. It implements a **focus set**—a group of foci—that can be requested together. This prevents part editors from generating a deadlock condition when each of several editors wants several foci.

Facets

A more complicated runtime issue, one that also relates to the allocation of resources among parts, is the notion of **facets**. In a graphical system that allows objects to be embedded within other objects, objects sometimes obscure (totally or partially) other objects. Objects that are totally obscured by other objects need not be drawn until their eclipsing object is moved aside. Likewise, these totally hidden objects are bypassed when keystrokes and mouse clicks are generated by the user.

OpenDoc maintains the complete hierarchy of parts and their embedded parts; this hierarchy is what is preserved in storage. At runtime, it is efficient to provide a parallel hierarchical structure that represents only the visible objects. Each visible part has a facet that is drawn and can receive events. Facets have links to their embedded facets directly; this facilitates the handling of commands and events.

Operations that relate to the ephemeral representation of parts on the screen (events, drawing, and so on), traverse the chain of facets. Operations that relate to the *content* of OpenDoc parts traverse the chain of parts and their embedded parts by using the visual representations of these parts (their frames). Only parts and frames are stored.

Facets are modified by their owning part editors which reflect modifications in their data elements (including their frames) in the visual representation of their facets as appropriate.

Data Transfer—Cut/Copy/Paste and Drag and Drop

Not only does OpenDoc allow a document to be composed of many different parts, it also allows information in one part to be copied or moved to another part. It is this aspect of OpenDoc that is often the most impressive to programmers. To users, it is a big yawn. Their reaction most often is that this is how they thought it should work all along.

Data transfer operations in OpenDoc are intuitive to the user, but listing them is a lengthy task. There are many combinations and permutations of cutting, copying, pasting, dragging, and dropping. This section takes a high-level approach to the matter, leaving the details to programming references. Fortunately, this approach is not unrealistic for the developer who is using ODF. Those parts of the data transfer operations not handled automatically by OpenDoc are mostly handled by ODF. The developer need write only the code specific to the part editor.

Guidelines for Data Transfer

The OpenDoc guidelines for data transfer rely on two aspects of all parts: their **part category** and their **part kind**. A part category describes the general type of data contained in a part. Categories are managed by CI Labs and include such types as plain text, styled text, movies, 2D graphics, 3D graphics, communications, databases, sounds, spreadsheets, and scripts (in the sense of OSA scripts). Part kinds are subdivisions of categories and reflect the specific part editor that operated last on that part's content. OpenDoc relies on kinds and categories in implementing data transfer.

Data transfer starts with the selection of something to be transferred. The selection may be a part (possibly containing other parts), or it may be all or part of the intrinsic content of the part (such as text, pictures, or a column in a spreadsheet). It may equally be intrinsic content with some embedded parts. It is the responsibility of the part editor to store all of the information necessary to complete the data transfer operation. The manner in which the data is transferred depends on the destination (which may not be determined by the user when the transfer starts), so the part editor (or ODF) generally must create several versions of the information in different part kinds so that any of several part editors may receive it.

Links

OpenDoc supports links between parts. Links enable changes made in one part to be reflected in another in real-time. The user may decide to complete the data transfer using a link, so the link must be able to be created in all cases where it is logical. For example, if the user is doing a Cut, a link could not exist from the soon-to-be-nonexistent cut information. The property kODPropLinkSpec is created by your part editor to support the potential creation of a link when the operation is completed.

Promises

Because parts may contain large amounts of data, OpenDoc incorporates the concept of **promises** that can be used in data transfer. The storage unit object method SetPromiseValue and the part method FulfillPromise let you implement promises. Note that the actual format of the promise data is private to the part editor; you may store anything you want in any format (including runtime pointers to objects that are transient).

Results of Data Transfer Operations

Data transfer operations rely on the number, kind, and category of the source and destination parts. The results of the operations are as follows. (In the first three cases, the selection is all or part of the intrinsic contents of a part.)

1. If the source is an intrinsic content of a part (such as selected text) and the destination is a part of the same kind (and thus of the same category), the data is **incorporated** into the second part. In other words, selecting a word in text editing part A and pasting it into text editing part B copies that word into the text stream in text editing part B.

2. If the circumstances are as in (1) but the destination part is of a different kind but a compatible category (*styled* text versus *unstyled* text), the data is **translated** and incorporated into the destination part. Thus copying *this text* from an editor that handles styled text into one that doesn't will paste "this text" in—as you would expect.

3. If the destination part is of an incompatible category (styled text versus sound), the selected information is **embedded**. A new part of the same kind and category as the source part is created, and the selected intrinsic information is placed in the new part. This new part is then embedded in the destination part.

In a sense, the philosophy behind the data transfer operations is minimalist: Do the smallest and simplest thing possible to carry out the user's wishes.

If the user has selected one or more parts (rather than intrinsic content), the rules for data transfer, again, are as simple as possible.

4. If a single part is selected, it is just embedded in the destination part (as the encapsulated part was embedded in (3) above).

5. If several parts are selected, their containing part enters into the picture. If the containing part is of the same category as the destination part's, the selected parts are simply embedded in the destination.

6. If several parts are selected and their container is of a different category than the destination part's, embedding them in the destination may be impossible. In this case, a new part of the same type as the container of the selected parts is created, encapsulating the selected parts. This encapsulated part is then embedded in the destination.

Of course, not all parts allow other parts to be embedded in them and not all parts allow all types of data to be transferred to them. The OpenDoc interface guidelines for each platform's implementation describe the feedback that should be given during drag and drop and cut/copy/paste operations so that the user cannot start on an operation that may fail.

> The easiest way to become familiar with OpenDoc's data transfer mechanism is to experiment with the sample parts provided on an OpenDoc CD-ROM.

Part Editor Runtime Integration

The last piece of the runtime puzzle is how OpenDoc actually puts the parts together and gets the code running. The specific implementation of this operation differs on each OpenDoc platform, but the basic principles are simple and the same. They consist of binding executable code to the instance data of a part and possibly translating a part.

Binding

When an OpenDoc part first needs to be used, OpenDoc binds an appropriate part editor to it. (Binding is not done for all parts in a document when it is opened; it is done on an as-needed basis.) The binding is based on the part's kind and category and on the user's preferences. In the simplest case, the same part editor that created the part and last edited it is used to display and edit it in the future.

In a more complex case, the original part editor is unavailable (either it has been removed or perhaps the document has been transferred to another environment). Part editors provide information about the kinds and categories of data that they can handle; parts provide information about the kind and category of data that they contain. OpenDoc makes the best match possible. In the worst case, a "part of last resort" is available that can display the part (if only as a gray shape at the appropriate location) and that can read and write—but not manipulate—the part's properties and values.

Users may explicitly set the editor for a part in the Part Info dialog box.

Alternative Representations

Part editors often store their data in alternative forms so that they are most likely to find an appropriate editor when the part is reopened. For example, a part editor might store data as both styled and unstyled text. When parts store their information in alternative representations, these representations are assumed to be stored in a sequence, in decreasing order of fidelity (best first).

Whether or not a part editor should store alternative representations of its data is a design issue that is usually easily decided. These representations may require more disk space and more processing time to maintain. In the case of part editors designed to run in a fairly controlled environment (within an enterprise, for example), such duplication may not be necessary. Part editors that are to be cast out into the world for use by many people in many environments may have several representations, so that as documents incorporating their parts move around, other editors can manipulate their data.

Translating

OpenDoc may require that the data in the part be translated for editing by a different type of editor. The user is invited to choose the kind and editor to which the part should be translated.

User Preferences

OpenDoc allows users to set preferences for editors of each kind and category. This allows a user to decide that, say, all text will be edited with part editor X and all bit-mapped graphics will be edited with part editor Y. The user preferences are used after OpenDoc has checked to see if the most preferred editor (the one last used on the part) is available.

Summary

The parts of the OpenDoc architecture discussed in this chapter are different on each platform. What they have in common is the commitment to making OpenDoc work as people expect it to and to making it unstoppable, that is, to prevent failures and to recover as easily as possible when they do occur. Problems that are the bane of the computer world (low memory and disk conditions, missing files, incompatible formats) are the bread-and-butter of the OpenDoc architecture.

One characteristic of OpenDoc shows through in all aspects of its architecture: It is a mature technology. It is mature not in the sense that it is old, but in the sense that it is wise, having profited from the experience of developers and users over the last half century. Things will fail. Users will attempt new tasks with old tools. Versions will be updated. Technology will change. Communications among computers will proliferate. OpenDoc lives in this world, not in a world of systems that work the way programmers wish they did.

OpenDoc's maturity is not dull or stultifying. It is not a closed system, trapping you into its notion of what you should be doing. It is open to change and experimentation. (Its container suite can be replaced, OSA can be replaced, and most OpenDoc objects can be overridden or modified with extensions.) In making OpenDoc open and exciting, this wisdom born of long years of struggle and frustration pays off.

In the next part of this book, the issues that OpenDoc poses for developers, users, consultants, and solution providers are presented. If the code samples in this part have been daunting, rest assured that the next part is code-free. In the final part, you'll see how to actually develop OpenDoc software and solutions. (There just might be a little bit of code there, though. . . .)

Part III

OpenDoc Issues

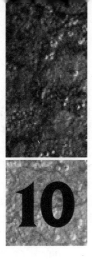

10

OpenDoc Issues
for Users

This chapter examines OpenDoc issues that are of interest to users and to computer managers, the people who are responsible for keeping users' computers running in larger organizations. You will see that there are only a few OpenDoc issues that affect users. For the most part, they are not new, but represent variations on existing issues with which users and managers are currently dealing. Why should users be concerned about OpenDoc at all? Some people feel it's only plumbing. But you'll see that OpenDoc does have benefits for users, especially when you see the effect it has on user interfaces and software usability. Some concerns have been raised about how OpenDoc software will be bought and sold. You will see that there is little reason for concern. Next you will see how OpenDoc simplifies the use and integration of different types of data. Many people are concerned about supporting software on multiple platforms, a concern OpenDoc was designed to address. After examining that issue, the issues of performance and memory usage, missing editors, and software configuration management are discussed.

OpenDoc Is the Best Plumbing

In recent years advertisements for plumbing fixtures have appeared even in upscale magazines such as *Gourmet* and *The New Yorker*. Plumbing that works well is never noticed; plumbing that works poorly is very obvious and becomes a major nuisance.

While OpenDoc is, for users, only plumbing, it is the best plumbing available. Users are not concerned with which APIs or development tools were used to create the software they are using, but they should be very concerned with how usable the software is. Software should be, but often isn't, easy to learn to use and easy to use (note that this is different from the previous item) and should allow the user to focus on the task at hand. Very few software packages meet these ideals. Obviously some software packages are better than others. OpenDoc provides a higher target that developers should aim for, while simultaneously providing a significant boost to the foundation on which software will be built. As a result of creating software that is closer to these ideals, developers will find that adopting OpenDoc will reduce the cost of supporting computer users. Users will also be pleased, since they will be able to focus on their own work and not how the software works (or doesn't).

Clarity of Function

The goal of most software developers is to develop software that will be perceived as "best of breed" and will be favorably reviewed in the trade press. One common aspect of the review in that press is a feature-by-feature comparison of the various products being reviewed. Developers have listened carefully to reviewers and consequently have gradually added more and more features. This is why the mainstream word processors have become desktop publishing packages over the last decade. As an unfortunate side effect of reviews and other business trends, pressures on developers have led to an "arms race," with the winner being the product with the most features as opposed to the product that enables its users to be most effective. There are few users today who use (or even know how to use) the majority of the features in their word processing or spreadsheet applications. This is the equivalent of the blinking clock on most people's VCRs. Why do users purchase upgrades, except for the need to read the latest (suddenly incompatible) file format from their friends and colleagues?

Large chunks of functions such as an index generator, table of contents generator, equation editor, and graph editor (none of which is core functionality for a word processing or spreadsheet application), have bloated monolithic applications. These functions, when added to standard horizontal applications, tend to receive less attention than the core product and consequently tend to be implemented in a mediocre manner. On the other hand, when they are implemented as separate applications, users have a hard time integrating them with their other applications. As an example, developers of bibliography software have a miserable time keeping up with the banalities of binary file formats. This problem would be eliminated, for the most part, in an OpenDoc world.

Developers have had to make many compromises in order to develop "best of breed" software, and users suffer because of it. Word processors should not contain code for creating tables and outlines, index generation, table of contents generation, and so on. These features are not core features needed in a word processor; they are used by only a small percentage of users, only part of the time. The interfaces of such applications become opaque to users because the software has become too complex.

In an OpenDoc world, these functions will become parts in their own right, independent of the core word processor. Users who want them can purchase them; users who don't will not have them cluttering up their hard disks. The developer of the core product can focus on producing the best word processor with the best interface and best performance without being distracted by adding hundreds of other features. Users will find that an OpenDoc word processor will have great clarity of function. An OpenDoc part editor is easier to use and to learn than its equivalent monolithic application. An OpenDoc part editor also will tend to have fewer bugs, since it has less source code and is less complex inside.

Changes in User Interfaces

OpenDoc does bring some user interface changes, however. Users will welcome them, if they notice them at all. Menus, windows, and dialog boxes behave as always. However, because the user can work in a task-centric manner under OpenDoc, the user no longer has to switch from application to application, cutting and pasting data from one to the other. Rather, the user interacts with the current document, dragging new parts from another window. The menu and tool palettes switch to reflect the type of the part which the user is currently working on.

According to usability tests conducted by Apple's OpenDoc human interface group, users feel OpenDoc provides a more natural, more intuitive way of interacting with software. Granted, this is a "soft" issue. But in today's environment, in which users training and support costs are equal to or more than the acquisition cost of the hardware and software, this advantage of OpenDoc makes financial sense, too. (For developers, too, the cost of supporting their software is often greater than the cost of developing it.)

There are well-defined user interface guidelines for each platform on which OpenDoc runs. These guidelines have been tested in usability labs to ensure they are an improvement. As long as OpenDoc developers follow these guidelines, which are extensions to the existing platform-specific interface guidelines, users will quickly and easily learn to use new part editors.

Users Find OpenDoc More Natural

Apple Computer did a number of usability tests to verify the user interface changes considered for OpenDoc. An interesting result was that some users did not notice the specific changes that were made. They did say, however, that "it seemed that a lot of bugs were fixed," meaning primarily that they felt much more comfortable with OpenDoc.

It is clear that users have less work to do when using OpenDoc than when using applications. Users do not have to keep track of the many different files that are to be combined into a single report. When using applications, users have to create graphics in one program, charts in another, tables in a third, and the report in a fourth. When using OpenDoc, all of the information lives in a single document, regardless of its type, and can be edited in place. Users will no longer have to transfer data from one document to another simply because it is the only way to combine different data types into a single document. Nor will they have to consciously switch from one application to another in order to exchange data or endure the half minute to minute it takes to launch another monolithic application.

And how many spell checkers do you really need, especially given that each has its own dictionary plus a file of words that you have added, and none of them can be moved into any other dictionary? How many address books do you need? You probably have several—in your PIM, e-mail, contact management, and groupware applications. With OpenDoc, you'll be able to live with a single spell checker and dictionary and with a single address book.

Plugging and Playing with Software

OpenDoc brings "plug and play" into the realm of software. CI Labs has a certification process for OpenDoc part editors. Hence mixing and matching part editors is relatively safe, since the "wiring" used to connect them to other editors has already been tested. Thirty years ago, consumer electronics, such as your dad's hi-fi set, were built as hefty pieces of furniture, with a radio, a record player, perhaps a reel-to-reel tape player, and a pair of well-endowed speakers. Consumer electronics have evolved a lot over the last several decades. Today, higher-quality consumer electronics are (with some exceptions) sold as components. You might purchase an amplifier (with tubes if you're really cool), a CD player, a cassette tape deck, a record player, an FM receiver, a television, and one or more sets of speakers. You might purchase them from one vendor, or you might mix and match by purchasing different components from different vendors. You don't worry about whether they can all be connected to one another or whether they can all work together. You know that there are standard types of connectors and cables, standard signal levels, and so on that all manufacturers use. In the same way, OpenDoc part editors can be connected together and you don't have to worry about whether they will work together.

Purchasing OpenDoc Parts

The advent of component software has brought both hopes and fears regarding software sales and distribution channels. Early discussions of how component software (including OpenDoc part editors) might be sold and distributed focused on more leading-edge scenarios. One scenario was the transition to a completely electronic mechanism for the sale and distribution of software through on-line services (such as Prodigy and America Online) or through the Internet. Other speculations included the extinction of the current sales and distribution channel.

As component software has become real, once again it has become obvious that all large systems, including the software sales and distribution channel, have inertia and tend to evolve to support changes in order to survive rather than make revolutionary changes. As it turns out, OpenDoc will not bring about radical changes in how software is sold and distributed. Distributors will continue to purchase boxes of software from software publishers and sell them to stores, which in turn will sell them to customers. OpenDoc part editors and suites of part editors will be sold in boxes on the shelves of stores just as applications are sold today.

Nevertheless, as the Internet and on-line services continue to grow, they will have a larger effect on how software is sold and distributed. CI Labs and the OpenDoc platform vendors are already experimenting with on-line catalogs and directories of OpenDoc parts. Other experiments are happening with software distribution and sales on encrypted CD-ROMs. OpenDoc does not pose any problems to any of these new mechanisms and is, in fact, quite compatible with them.

Cross-Platform Support

Organizations of any substantial size usually have several different platforms—such as Windows, Macintosh, OS/2, UNIX—on their collective desktops. Locating applications—except the basic horizontal ones—that run on multiple platforms is difficult. Even if a vendor supports more than one platform, support for some platforms often lags behind others, sometimes by as much as a year.

From the start, OpenDoc was envisioned as a cross-platform architecture. It is supported on Windows, Macintosh, OS/2, and UNIX today, and some vendors are considering porting it to additional platforms. Already there are some OpenDoc development tools that support several of these platforms. These tools include IBM's Open Class Library, Apple's OpenDoc Development Framework (ODF), and Oracle's Power Objects. Others are expected in the near future. As developers create new OpenDoc part editors using these tools, users can expect to see part editors available on several, if not all, OpenDoc platforms simultaneously. The demand for cross-platform solutions is one of the driving forces behind OpenDoc.

Integration of Different Types of Data

The development of the clipboard metaphor in support of cut, copy, and paste commands enabled users to combine different types of data together in a single document. A user can paste a drawing into a word processing document or paste some text from a word processor into a speech synthesizer. However, the responsibility for supporting each data type falls on each application. The minor (and sometimes major) problems every computer user experiences when copying and pasting data arise from the increasingly large number of data types that have to be supported by each application.

The number of data types that need to be supported continues to grow at a rapid pace. When a new data type becomes popular, then the application developer must write new code to support it. In the last several years, users have gotten used to VRML (Virtual Reality Markup Language), Apple QuickTime movies, and Apple QuickTime/Virtual Reality (QT-VR) movies. They've also become accustomed to URLs (uniform reference locations as used on the Internet) and new types of audio files (such as DSP Group's TrueSpeech compressed audio that allows real-time transmission and reception of audio over the Internet). As the average bandwidth of communications channels increases and the average clock speed and memory capacity of computers increase, even more data types will be created. Updates to support new data types must fit into product release cycles, which are getting longer and longer because of the complexity of applications. Users become frustrated because it may take a year before they see a version that supports the new data type with which they want to work. And when the new version supporting that one exciting data type arrives, it is laden with a multitude of other new features—often of no interest to the user.

OpenDoc makes the integration of data types much easier because that is one of its primary design goals. While OpenDoc part editors are often designed to work with a single data type, almost all can have other parts with different types of content embedded within them. Users who are working with OpenDoc parts will find that they are copying and pasting less than before, but dragging and dropping more often. When a new data type arrives, then the user needs a part editor for that data type. The user can then embed the data type in any OpenDoc document, regardless of how old the document is or how few data types it contains. There is a price to pay for supporting new data types with OpenDoc; however, it is small compared with that of doing it with monolithic applications.

Performance and Memory Usage

Users and developers may have some concerns regarding memory usage and performance of OpenDoc part editors. Those fears are unfounded. OpenDoc part editors are simpler and smaller than equivalent applications, so they will take up less space on disk as well as less memory when executed.

The time required to launch a part editor will also be significantly less. In fact, the OpenDoc runtime environment generally tries to hide the times when part editors are launched or shut down. The goal is that users not be conscious of when these events occur. The OpenDoc environment must also manage the seamless passing of events between part editors when users shift focus from one part to another. The OpenDoc platform vendors have tried especially hard to optimize the transition of control from one editor to another in order to provide a high-quality user experience.

Missing Part Editors

One concern about OpenDoc has to do with when a user receives a document containing a part for which he or she does not have a suitable part editor or viewer. To understand why this is a concern, you need to understand how OpenDoc handles a part that has a type. When the OpenDoc runtime environment is presented with a new type of part, it tries first to find a part editor or viewer that can handle the format and type of the data. If that attempt fails, it then can try to find an alternative part editor or viewer that can translate the part's type of data into something it can use. In the worst possible case, OpenDoc will display a gray region indicating the "mystery" part's location and size to the user. The user can then query the part to find out what part editor was used to edit it. This is actually better than the current situation with applications. If a user receives a file for which he or she does not have the application used to create it, he or she may not even be able to learn what kind of file it is.

OpenDoc developers are encouraged to store data in multiple formats within a document as one means of reducing this problem. This makes it easier for a user receiving a document to be able to edit it, or at least view it. Developers have also been encouraged to support data format translations as another means of dealing with this problem.

OpenDoc developers are also encouraged to distribute free part viewers so that users do not need to purchase additional software in order to simply read or print a document. The OpenDoc architects decided that OpenDoc editors and viewers should not be distributed with the documents that use them because of the danger of computer viruses and other security risks. Otherwise that might have been a reasonable solution in some circumstances.

Configuration Management

Configuration management is an issue that confronts all organizations today. If each user purchases his or her own software without regard for corporate standards, the cost to provide technical support, appropriate computer and network configurations, and upgrades can quickly grow beyond the capabilities of the organization.

OpenDoc does not eliminate the need for configuration management. Just as users can keep multiple versions of a software package or use an alternative word processor, users can keep multiple versions of a part editor or use alternative editors. Organizations that have centralized policies on the usage of software will need to make only minor revisions to incorporate part editors and stationery.

Summary

As should be obvious by now, users and microcomputer managers should have few, if any, problems in making a transition to Open-Doc. Most users, especially home and small office users, may not even be aware that they are using OpenDoc as opposed to monolithic applications. Overall, OpenDoc users should find that their new software is easier to use, requires less support, and allows them to focus on their tasks instead of the software they use.

OpenDoc software will tend to be sold in the same manner and through the usual channels in which you purchase software today. As software distribution and sales channels evolve, perhaps to include electronic and CD-ROM-based channels, OpenDoc software will follow. Cross-platform development is strongly supported by the OpenDoc architecture, since that was one of its design goals. As a compound document architecture, OpenDoc naturally supports the continually increasing number of data types.

Users of OpenDoc software should not find any problems with performance or memory requirements. Users should face fewer obstacles with missing part editors and with applications that cannot read incompatible files because OpenDoc developers have been encouraged to provide several different solutions to these problems. Finally, OpenDoc does not change the status quo with respect to configuration management. Computer managers will still have to deal with this issue.

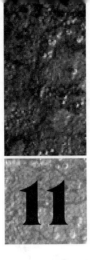

11

OpenDoc Technical Issues for Developers

This chapter provides a look at technical issues that affect Open-Doc software developers, including software publishers, systems integrators, value-added resellers (VARs) and in-house developers. While both OpenDoc and object-oriented programming provide a means for managing the complexities of software development, OpenDoc has a mechanism for managing a higher order of complexity. Moving your current code base to OpenDoc is a relatively straightforward process—OpenDoc was designed to be integrated into a world of existing software. For example, Open-Doc works well in a distributed computing environment and is also well-suited for developing database and accounting software. These issues are the substance of this chapter.

OpenDoc and Object-Oriented Programming

The increasing complexity of operating systems and interfaces has driven the increased use of object-oriented languages and application frameworks for the development of monolithic applications. OpenDoc parts can be created with object-oriented languages and frameworks, although developers can still use procedural languages, too. There are other choices for OpenDoc development tools besides programming languages, such as 4GL tools like Oracle's Power Objects.

The Increasing Complexity of Operating Systems

In the early days of microcomputers, there were at most several hundred API calls available in the first-generation microcomputer operating systems such as Digital Research's CP/M, the Apple II DOS, and Microsoft DOS. Developers on desktop and workstation platforms confront operating system API sets that now contain thousands of calls. Life was easy for programmers, but users had to work hard. The rise of graphical user interfaces shifted some of the burden from users to programmers.

Today all operating system vendors are in the process of growing both the breadth and depth of their operating systems by including massive amounts of functionality in order to differentiate their platforms. In earlier years, an application developer would have to have developed these functions from scratch or licensed them in the form of a third-party code library. This trend of adding large chunks of functionality seems like it will continue into the foreseeable future. The industry passed the time some years ago when a single programmer could comprehend an entire operating system in detail.

The recent rise of interest in object-oriented programming languages is directly related to this trend. Frameworks have provided some relief for application developers because they abstract standard platform behaviors, thereby allowing developers to focus on their application's unique functions and behaviors. Frameworks have shifted some of the burden from application developers to framework developers.

The Increasing Complexity of User Interfaces

As already said, developers now deal with sophisticated graphical user interfaces that are designed to make life easier for users, but which make the work of the developer harder. Developers are expected to create interfaces that are easy to learn, easy to use (by novice and expert users), intuitive, flexible, and so on. Given the large size of the operating system API set and users' acceptance and enforcement of user interface guidelines, developers have found it difficult to create an interface that satisfies user expectations and interface guidelines by using a procedural language. This is not to say it cannot be done. There is no question that a developer using C or Pascal can create and maintain an interface. However, the burden of dealing with the complexity of the interface and the API fall squarely on the shoulders of the developer. A better use of the developer's time is to work on the unique functions of the application.

Figure 11-1 illustrates how the burdens of computing have gradually changed. In the first column, you can see that in the days of the early desktop systems the operating system (OS) did relatively little. The programmer, while working hard, still had it easier than the user. In the second column, you can see that as later operating

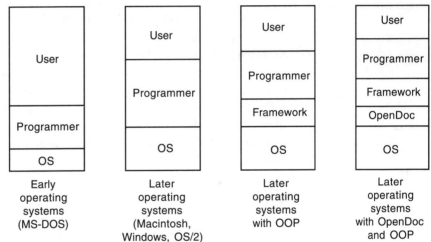

Figure 11-1.

Who bears the burdens of computing?

systems evolved to include graphical user interfaces (Macintosh, Windows, and OS/2), the operating system began doing a lot more, the users began doing less, but programmers were working very hard. In the third column, the programmer's job gets a little easier with the introduction of object-oriented programming (OOP) and application frameworks. Users also benefit because frameworks support a greater level of consistency with user interface guidelines and allow developers to spend more time improving the user interface. Finally, in the fourth column, OpenDoc brings benefits to both programmers and users.

In the world of component software, object-oriented languages and frameworks are undoubtedly the preferred way to start new projects or, in some cases, to port existing code from applications into components. There are many developers, however, who have existing applications that were written using procedural languages such as C, Pascal, and Fortran. Their code can be brought into OpenDoc part editors, too.

Using Procedural Languages to Create OpenDoc Part Editors

Developers can develop OpenDoc part editors using non-object-oriented languages, including C or Pascal, since the OpenDoc APIs do not require the use of an object-oriented language. The OpenDoc APIs are based on SOM technology and use an IDL to isolate developers from the OpenDoc implementation. Using a procedural language, however, forces the developer to deal directly with the OpenDoc APIs, which is a less attractive option than using a part editor framework. Given the realities of the software market, if you are developing an OpenDoc part editor from scratch, don't use a procedural language. The advantages of object-oriented languages still have a good payback in the development of components.

Some Curious Facts About C++

An interesting side note on C++ is that many industry observers, including market research firms, have exaggerated the growth of C++. Virtually all compiler vendors have migrated their products to C++, so there really aren't any C compilers left to buy. If you simply look at sales of C++ compilers or the number of programmers who use C++ compilers, you don't really know whether the programmers are using C++ or that proper subset of C++ known as C. Many C++ programmers are still writing in C.

Also interesting is that while C++ is an object-oriented language that has significant benefits over its procedural predecessor, paradoxically, when coupled with a framework, C++ code is generally less portable than C code. C code tends to be bound to the operating system API(s) for which it was written. C++ code tends to be bound to a framework and to an operating system API set. C++ and C code can be written in a portable manner, but writing portable C++ code is more difficult. The moral is to choose your framework very carefully—you'll be living with for a long time.

Developers Have Other Choices

Developers have other choices besides object-oriented and procedural languages. Oracle's Power Objects is one example. Another is Novell's AppWare development environment, which will support the development of OpenDoc parts. These tools are easier to learn to use than C++ and, for some developers and projects, are far more appropriate.

OpenDoc and Software Complexity

Just as operating systems have become complex, so have applications. The larger applications you use may contain more than a million lines of code. Applications have become too complex.

The Increasing Complexity of Function within Applications

The user's expectations for application software have soared over the last 10 years, thus requiring the monolithic applications to become increasingly more complex. As discussed earlier, the time has passed when a programmer could fully understand a complete operating system. Similarly, the time has passed when one programmer could fully understand all of the source code for a single (large) application. This means that while a single programmer can conceive of and design a monolithic application, it is increasingly less likely that a single programmer can write all of the code for it and then maintain it afterwards. The days when a single programmer can create a best-selling application are dwindling, if they haven't disappeared completely, because the economics of software development and of the monolithic application marketplace make it very difficult for a lone programmer to compete.

Object-Oriented Programming Helps Developers Manage Complexity

Over the last 10 years, there has been a rise of the new trend in software development called object-oriented programming. Object-oriented programming has enabled programmers to develop and maintain software that is significantly larger and more complex than was possible using procedural languages. Object-oriented languages have enabled this because they provide mechanisms for managing complexity, thereby reducing the workload of developers.

Application Frameworks

The most reasonable way to program with an object-oriented language is to use an application framework, a collection of classes that implement the standard and basic features expected of an application on the platforms it supports. One design goal of frameworks is to abstract many details of the underlying operating system into classes so that the application programmer does not need to understand them.

Generally it is not easy to fit an entire application written in a procedural language into an application framework. It is usually too large of a shift in technology, although in many cases it is possible to move some code. Moving a lot of procedural code into a framework means there would be relatively few benefits from using the new object-oriented language or framework. Monolithic applications cannot be moved into a framework without a complete rewrite of the application; the structural complexities of an application usually don't map well onto a framework.

While some developers have created their own frameworks, there is much risk associated with this path, as opposed to using a commercial, off-the-shelf framework. This is for several reasons. First, if the developers have not done sufficient object-oriented programming, the risk of failure is quite high. Second, frameworks can be thought of as a layer of system software. They must, at some level, be tightly bound to at least one operating system, since one of their purposes is to reduce the complexity of application development.

This leads to two modes in which the process of developing a new framework can fail: failing to understand the full range of services that the framework must service and failing to track advances in the platform API(s). Third, the cost of developing and maintaining the framework must be added to the overall application development costs. Only a handful of companies might be able to afford the costs of developing an application framework.

The good news for monolithic application developers is that there are many frameworks to choose from. There are single platform frameworks, such as Microsoft's MFC (Windows), Borland's OWL (two versions, one for Windows and the other for OS/2), Metrowerks' PowerPlant (Macintosh), and Apple's MacApp (Macintosh). There are also more than a dozen frameworks that support more than one platform, including Visix's Galaxy and XVT Software's XVT.

While application frameworks have helped to manage the complexity of application software, the bad news is they create problems of their own. Large application frameworks are used to create large monolithic applications, but the resulting code base becomes too rigid when there are more than several hundred thousand lines of code. Making significant changes to an application that has a million lines of code written on top of an application framework is harder than it should be, given how strongly the benefits of object-oriented programming have been touted.

Component Software Is the Next Evolutionary Step

As should be clear by now, object-oriented programming languages and application frameworks have enabled significant advances in application development over the use of procedural languages. In fact, the predominant mode for developing software today is to develop monolithic applications using an object-oriented language and a framework. Nevertheless, the industry is reaching new limits of complexity with this technology. When an application is implemented as tens of megabytes of source code, in the form of hundreds of classes, the code base has become too complex. It takes too long to add new features, to fix bugs, and to get that next revision out the door.

What are you to do? Component software is the next step in the management of software complexity. C++, CLOS (Common Lisp Object System), Smalltalk, and Dylan are all excellent object-oriented languages in their own ways, but they provide a solution to the *initial* type of complexity that developers confront. Object-oriented languages by themselves do not solve all types of software complexity.

The next level of software complexity can be managed by moving to component software. By separating the functions provided by a large monolithic application, you might end up with five to 10 software components. Each component would have a clear, well-focused purpose and much less code than the application would. Once again, it will be possible for a single programmer to be able to conceive of, design, and implement a nontrivial piece of software. This won't always happen because some components, such as a core word processor, will still be large. However, a word processor component will still be significantly smaller and less complex than the monolithic word processors of today.

Jumping from monolithic applications to components is analogous to the transition from CISC (Complex Instruction Set Computer) to RISC (Reduced Instruction Set Computer) in microprocessors. As it turns out, the complexity of a RISC chip, as measured by the equivalent number of transistors, is not a tenth of a comparable CISC chip, but only a third or a quarter. The next generation of RISC chip is both easier and quicker to design than the next generation of CISC chip. Similarly, because the complexity of a component is less than that of the equivalent application, a component will be able to evolve more quickly than an application.

Frameworks for OpenDoc Part Editors

The OpenDoc equivalent to an application framework is a part editor framework. Four frameworks are available now and others are under development. IBM offers a framework that ships along with its CSet++ compiler called the Open Class Library, available on both for OS/2 and AIX. IBM is planning to port it to Macintosh and Windows as well. Apple has developed the OpenDoc Development Framework, a cross-platform framework that will initially support OpenDoc on Macintosh and Windows but is being ported to OS/2 and AIX. Two Macintosh C++ compiler vendors are extending their Macintosh-only frameworks to support OpenDoc: Metrowerks with the PowerPlant framework and Symantec with the Think Class Library.

Object-oriented programming has helped manage some of the complexity of software, but it is clearly not the "silver bullet" of software engineering. The migration to software components, in turn, is not a panacea for all software development ills, since it cannot manage all remaining levels of complexity. There are other tools for managing complexity at higher levels of organization.

Preparing Your Code for the Transition

The choice of making a transition from monolithic applications to component software is an important question all developers will face in the next several years. Perhaps the most difficult question is what to do about your existing code base. Your decision should be based on many factors, including the current state of your code base (whether it still has some life left or has become too fragile for additional development), your market position, the state of your development staff, and your future plans for your products.

Your have three options:

1. Start over and create new OpenDoc part editors from scratch.
2. Convert your application into a set of OpenDoc part editors.
3. Convert your application into a container application, which is examined in more detail in the following discussion.

The first option may be optimal if you look at it purely from a technical point of view, but for some developers it is not an option. In some cases, this option may be too expensive; in others, it may be expensive, but worth it. Small developers who are willing to go for this option may end up in a great position in the marketplace. Large developers may need to make a large investment in order to get into the component software marketplace but may be able to leap over their competitors in doing so. Whether they do this will depend on the market position they want to stake out. By rethinking the purpose of their products, developers will be able to move away from bloated products toward well-focused, well-designed, well-implemented software that will be well received by customers.

The second option provides some middle ground between your old code base and component software. Before you do anything, think through what your core product should do and how you will break up the functions in your current application(s) into components. You may discover that there are some components that are not essential to your business and that it may be less expensive in the long run to license those part editors from other companies rather than redevelop them yourself.

Depending on how your software is structured, you may be able to separate core functions as "engines" that can be moved into an OpenDoc part editor or extension. Then your next task is to develop a new user interface. If this approach is not feasible, you should then consider isolating small pieces of functionality and rebuilding them into part editors. If this is not possible, then you should reconsider the first and third options.

Container Applications

When you are starting with an existing code base, the simplest way to get started with OpenDoc development is to turn your application into a container application. A container application behaves like a root OpenDoc part. Other OpenDoc parts can be embedded within the root, but it can never be embedded within another part. To make your application into a container application, you must modify it to be able to make direct OpenDoc API calls in the appropriate places. This is not much work, and the payoff is, your application can quickly find a place in the OpenDoc world. Doing this also gives you experience developing with OpenDoc.

The largest disadvantage is that your new container application is still an application. Your application has even more code than before (since you've had to add some OpenDoc calls), so it takes just as long to launch and offers only modest benefits with respect to OpenDoc. All things considered, transforming your application into a container application should be thought of as a short-term step in preparation for a full-scale transition to OpenDoc.

To be a container application, your application should do the following, at a minimum:

1. Act like a simple containing part. Your container application should at a minimum support the basic requirements for being able to contain parts. For example, it does not need to support frame size negotiation. On the other hand, it should be able to embed multiple parts. The container application should behave like a real, but perhaps extremely limited, root part.

2. Act like a simple document shell by creating an OpenDoc runtime environment and managing both its own and the OpenDoc environment. Events that belong to the application should be handled as before, but those that belong to a part must be passed to the OpenDoc environment. This is also true for drawing and disk storage.

3. Properly handle both the usual errors as well as OpenDoc-related errors.

Macintosh Container Applications

Macintosh developers using C, Pascal, or C++ have an alternative if they want to make their applications into container applications. Apple Computer has developed a library with a procedural API, known as CALib (for Container Application Library). Programmers can use CALib to quickly and easily turn their application into a container application just by making a few calls to this library.

Apple's goal in creating CALib is to make it easy for application programmers to allow the embedding of OpenDoc parts without their having to learn the OpenDoc API set. A container application also does not have to support the Drag and Drop Manager, the Edition Manager (used for OpenDoc linking), or the AOCE Mailer in order to use this library. To use CALib, an application cannot use the Bento services or support linking to native content.

CALib works by creating a proxy part that represents the root, as well as a proxy root frame and proxy root facet. The proxy part contains all embedded parts in the container application's content, does trivial frame negotiation for embedded parts (requests for shape changes and additional frames are always refused), and manages the root frame (which is the entire application's document window). This part is provided as a part editor.

MacApp developers have it even easier, since Apple is developing a new version of MacApp (version 3.5) that will have CALib support built into the application framework. MacApp has been the predominant application framework used by Macintosh programmers.

Programmers on platforms other than the Macintosh who are interested in developing container applications may want to look into CALib. Apple will be distributing source to CALib and the Proxy part.

Distributed Computing

OpenDoc very naturally supports distributed computing and client/server architecture. One of the foundations of OpenDoc is the System Object Model (SOM) and the Distributed System Object Model (DSOM) extensions to it. SOM was developed by IBM to solve several problems. First, it solves the problem of allowing software modules written in different languages to interoperate. Using SOM, a COBOL program can call a C module, which can then use a C++ object to perform some computation. SOM also enables developers to distribute code libraries without source code. Second, SOM (actually the DSOM flavor) solves the problem of how a module running on one computer can talk with module running on another computer.

Even without SOM, there is nothing in OpenDoc that is not compatible with distributed computing. With the OpenDoc extension mechanism, it is possible to abstract the details of a particular type of network connection or transaction protocol so that the part editors are independent of them.

Database and Accounting Applications

Database management systems (DBMS) and accounting software are two examples of software that are not document-centric. Until recently, the interface guidelines for various platforms focused primarily on document-centric software, such as word processors, graphics and spreadsheets. As a result, the quality of the user interfaces has tended to suffer somewhat, since platform vendors have done little interface design research for these types of software. Also, until recently application frameworks have tended to reflect the document-centric concerns of standard horizontal applications such as spreadsheets, word processors, and drawing programs. Fortunately, both interface guidelines and frameworks have broadened in recent years to better support a wider range of software.

Even though the OpenDoc name obviously was derived from "document," the OpenDoc architecture provides an excellent platform for creating software such as accounting systems and front-end components for DBMSs. As already mentioned, OpenDoc gives you an architectural method of separating a large complex application into a set of software components. Database engines, which underlie both a DBMS and an accounting system, should probably still be implemented as stand-alone applications or libraries running in their own address spaces, communicating with OpenDoc parts. However, the various front-ends, such as general ledger, accounts payable, and so on for an accounting package and query and report writers, form designers, and so on for a DBMS could well be implemented as OpenDoc part editors.

User Interface Issues

This section briefly covers several user interface issues that developers should be aware of: the role of stationery, handling content from non-OpenDoc software, and linking.

The Role of Stationery

Stationery—the duplication of a document template to give the user a head start—has been around for only a few years on the various desktop platforms. It has not been widely used by either developers or users. Application developers tend to provide sample documents instead of stationery. In the OpenDoc world, however, stationery plays a much larger role. Users will not be starting applications as they do today; rather they will open a stationery document to create a new document and drag other stationery documents into their documents to add new types of content. As a result, OpenDoc developers should think about the role of stationery in their software. Stationery can be used by developers to add value to their product; for example, they could create different stationery documents in order to provide a wide range of templates. Consider providing different stationery for novice users and experienced users or specialized stationery for vertical markets.

Content from Non-OpenDoc Sources

Users can paste content that has been copied from non-OpenDoc sources, such as applications. If the data type of the content to be pasted is the same as that of the intrinsic content of your part, then the pasted content should be merged with the current part content. If it is not, then it should be embedded as a separate part.

Linking

Linking, under the OpenDoc user interface guidelines, is treated as a special case of pasting rather than as a separate command. One improvement OpenDoc offers developers in this area is that Clipboard support (cut, copy, and paste), linking, and drag and drop support are all handled in the same way. Previously each of these cases was handled slightly differently on each of the various OpenDoc platforms.

Scripting

The scripting capabilities supported by the Open Scripting Architecture (OSA) of OpenDoc give systems integrators and in-house developers a powerful mechanism for integrating Open-Doc components together to create new systems out of them. OSA is not a scripting language, but rather an architecture for scripting languages to be plugged into. On OS/2, the scripting languages are REXX and BASIC. On Windows, the language is BASIC. On Macintosh, it is AppleScript. Scripting is discussed at length in Chapter 8.

Summary

This chapter examined OpenDoc issues that are of interest to developers. The first topic was the relationship between OpenDoc and object-oriented programming. OpenDoc part editors can be developed using object-oriented programming languages, procedural languages, 4GLs, and other tools. Like object-oriented programming, OpenDoc has provided a solution for managing the complexity of software, albeit at a higher level. This benefit of OpenDoc may be the most significant for many developers.

Next, you read about the three options for moving your code base to OpenDoc part editors: starting from scratch, breaking your application into a set of OpenDoc part editors, and making an application into a container application. The next topic was the suitability of OpenDoc for distributing a computing environment and for handling non-document-centric applications such as for database management systems and accounting. The last two topics examined were some OpenDoc user interface issues and the scripting of OpenDoc part editors.

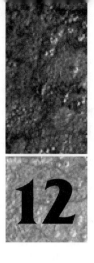

12 OpenDoc Business Issues for Developers

This chapter looks at business issues that are of interest to Open-Doc software developers, including software publishers, systems integrators, VARs and in-house developers. The topics examined are the economics of the commercial software business, how to prepare your organization to make the transition to OpenDoc and the world of component software, and licensing opportunities.

Economics of the Commercial Software Business

The basic trend of the last several years is disheartening to many in the software industry: While the costs of developing commercial software packages are rising, prices of software are falling. For example, the price of a word processor has dropped steadily over the last five years. A large factor in this trend has been the rise of application suites.

When the concept of application suites was first marketed, such suites sold for a small discount over the total cost of the applications contained within the suite. Gradually, then faster, prices for suites have dropped so that you can now purchase an entire suite of applications for the same amount of money that a word processor cost only a few years earlier. In 1995, there were only three significant vendors of application suites: Microsoft, Novell (through its purchase of WordPerfect), and IBM (through its purchase of Lotus). The market positions of the latter two are tenuous. As a direct result of the change in the economics of the software industry, there has been a major wave of consolidations and mergers. This has reduced the number of major software vendors and virtually eliminated small developers who were competing in the horizontal software business.

Along with all of these changes, or perhaps because of them, the software industry is no longer driven by technology. Today, it is driven by marketing. Smaller software developers, unless they are backed by significant capital, have difficulty both developing their products and selling them in the market. There are always some exceptions, of course, but the software marketplace is very different than it was 10 years ago. While most people believe smaller developers are more innovative than large developers are, the chances of succeeding as a small developer seem to be dwindling.

OpenDoc may change the software industry so that small developers have a better chance of succeeding. Of course, large developers also would have more opportunities to succeed, but it will be easier for small developers to compete. Certain factors will make it even more difficult for large developers. For example, large organizations tend to take longer to make decisions. Also, their code bases are very large, and they have a lot of products. So they will find it somewhat harder to capitalize on OpenDoc than will small developers.

Suites will not disappear just because component software is becoming more significant in the software business. In fact, the rise of OpenDoc will encourage the growth of suites, since developers will be able to create customized suites. Instead of a "one size fits all" kind of suite for all users, publishers will be able to offer a suite for lawyers, another for engineers, a third for teachers, and so on. These new suites will contain a common subset of part editors as well as additional editors and resources (such as dictionaries) that are especially suited to a targeted set of customers. The customers, in turn, will be able to further modify their suite by purchasing (or developing) other part editors.

OpenDoc allows developers to focus on their core competencies. Rather than having to write code to support a new data type, such as maps or digital movies, OpenDoc developers will be able to add support by including another part editor with their package, perhaps one licensed from another developer.

All developers have to live within a budget. If you have the budget for five programmer years to spend on developing a piece of software, you are far better off spending the vast majority of them on functions that make a difference to *your* organization than spending only half of them on that and half on functions that every application must have. In this way, your mapping editor or word processor or other product has the possibility of standing out. Figure 12-1 illustrates how this could work. When you are developing an application, you must allocate a significant amount of time developing generic functionality. This is true even when you are using C++ and a framework. When you are developing a part editor, you can concentrate most of your efforts on what makes your software unique, thereby giving you an edge over other developers.

OpenDoc brings other marketing options. For example, you can implement specialized versions of your software that fit smaller niche markets than before because the development costs can be much less than before. Marketing and sales costs may not

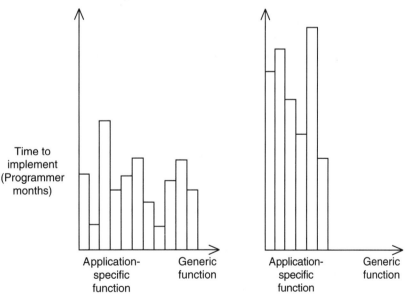

Figure 12-1.

Allocating developer time: application versus OpenDoc part editor

Time to implement (Programmer months)

Application-specific function — Generic function

Application: Budget = 21 programmer months

Application-specific function — Generic function

OpenDoc part editor: Budget = 21 programmer months

change, but the incremental revenues may make it quite profitable. For example, you might consider creating different versions of your editors to market to different splits in the market, catering to, say, different levels of expertise or different age levels or focusing on narrow slices of the market, such as sports or gardening or the construction industry. This contrasts with the current marketplace in which developers tend to sell—and resell—software and its upgrades to a single consumer base.

Preparing Your Organization for the Transition to OpenDoc

Making a successful transition in technology requires a good understanding of the pertinent issues, thorough planning, and good execution of the plan. Technology transitions are usually difficult because of a combination of technical and nontechnical reasons. For example, the transition from procedural languages such as C or COBOL to object-oriented languages such as C++ or Smalltalk is not quick; nor is it easy. Developers have to learn a new language, an application framework, a new way of debugging software, and a new way of designing software. Managers have to learn something of the language, new ways of managing development projects (since more design time is essential for successful object-oriented projects), new ways of managing their managers, new ways of testing software and, in some cases, new ways of working with customers. Note that there are technical and business (nontechnical) changes required to make a successful technology transition. If one or more aspects is neglected, then the transition may fail.

Similarly, your successful transition to component software using OpenDoc will require thought and care. Developers, their managers, and other members of your organization must be prepared for this transition. Most of these people will need some training in order to be able to think "components" instead of applications. In 1995, Apple Computer wanted to investigate how the component software market could be established. They hired a market research firm to conduct a platform-neutral study on this topic that included developers on Windows, Macintosh, and other platforms. The research firm talked with developers and managers who worked for software publishers, VARs, systems integrators, and enterprise organizations. It found that the number one technical barrier across all platforms and markets that was inhibiting the move to component software was the need for training.

Beyond that, shifting the industry towards component software is based on and requires standards that permit OpenDoc parts to be interoperable and/or interchangeable. This is accomplished with the OpenDoc architecture, and is ensured by CI Labs.

Preparing Developers for the Transition to OpenDoc

Developers will, of course, need training on OpenDoc concepts and development tools. All platform vendors and some third-party companies provide technical training courses on these topics. Depending on the background of the developer and the tools your organization will use for developing OpenDoc part editors, other training courses may be appropriate, including courses on object-oriented programming and design, platform API, and development tools.

Learning the technical aspects of OpenDoc is the easy part. Learning to think "components" is a little harder and requires that you step back and rethink how you conceive of and design software. Many programmers find it takes one, two, or even more projects working with object-oriented languages before they "get" it. Learning to think in terms of components is somewhat easier. However, transitions such as these are always easier if you can get advice from someone more experienced to get feedback about design and implementation issues. For this, your organization can either hire people or consultants with these skills.

Preparing Managers for the Transition to OpenDoc

Managers, like developers, will need training on OpenDoc concepts and technologies, although in less detail. Depending on their background and previous experience, they may need training in areas such as development tools, new development methods, and new ways of managing the software development process. For example, most developers report that projects using object technology require that you spend sufficient time doing the internal design work before proceeding with the implementation. Indeed, projects based on object technology tend to fail if insufficient time is spent on design. While time spent on design is also important for projects using procedural languages, such projects are less vulnerable to failure if the design time is skimpy than are object-oriented projects. If the managers in your organization expect developers to spend most of their time in front of a computer typing in code, then their expectations need to be reset.

The transition to component software will undoubtably require changes to the processes your organization uses to develop software, especially if you will be using new development tools. Projects using new technology should be selected carefully and should be appropriate for the tools you plan to use. Expectations for the new technology should be set appropriately for all levels within your organization.

Preparing Your Business for the Transition to OpenDoc

The people responsible for developing your business strategy and for the marketing of your products or services will need to understand how OpenDoc will change your long-term technical strategies. OpenDoc and the transition to component software presents several interesting opportunities.

First, whenever a major transition occurs, companies that can better take advantage of the new opportunities to jump into the new model have the chance to leap over existing competitors and establish a new market position. Of course, not all transitions are successful, nor are all companies that make the jump successful in either the business or the technical sense. As already mentioned, existing technology (monolithic applications) seems to be reaching an upper limit. Major transitions in technology do not happen every year. Consider whether this transition to component software is one on which your organization should capitalize now.

Second, at a minimum, component software does offer an opportunity to change the economics of software development. Given the ease with which OpenDoc part editors can be combined, it is much easier to either license parts from other companies or outsource their development.

The OEM Market for OpenDoc Part Editors

Developers, especially in-house developers and systems integrators, will be able to focus on the core technologies that will differentiate them from others. Instead of having to develop all parts, you can now consider licensing parts from other companies or outsourcing their development. Licensing will likely increase, since OpenDoc parts can be used in concert with less chance of incompatibilities.

Once you have developed part editors, you should consider licensing them yourself as a way of recouping your investment in the part's development and maintenance. This opportunity is available even to organizations that do not participate as a software or systems vendor. If your organization falls into this camp, and has no interest in participating, then you might consider establishing a relationship with another company that could do sales, support, and even additional development in exchange for royalties or other considerations.

Summary

This chapter covered the business issues that affect OpenDoc developers, regardless of the organization in which they work. First you saw how OpenDoc brings the possibility of changing the industry so that small innovative developers once again can have a significant effect on the software business. Second, you read about how to prepare your organization for the OpenDoc transition and about licensing opportunities.

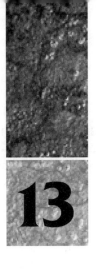

13

One Size Fits One: The Business Case for Component Software

By Robert P. Beech, President and CEO,
Pharos Technologies, Inc.

For a given industry, customers for vertical market software will have many common requirements, plus a number of unique requirements that are of high business value. Historically, customers have been forced to choose a totally custom solution to satisfy all of their requirements. Component-based software will help provide the entire spectrum of customer requirements, while dramatically reducing the time, cost, and development risks normally associated with custom software.

Prefabricated Building Blocks

Components can best be described as the software equivalent of prefabricated building blocks. Distinct from software objects, components are larger modules, built from a number of tightly integrated objects, that represent a much higher level of functionality. Properly architected components can be readily assembled to provide a partial or complete software solution. In many ways, software components are analogous to hardware's integrated circuit chips, with the important difference that software "chips" can be more easily modified and customized.

Components represent an opportunity to reuse large amounts of code, in different combinations, to satisfy the common and uncommon requirements of specific markets. This includes the ability to combine and reuse components that have been fabricated by different development sources. With the advent of Open-Doc and OLE, industry-wide component standards are taking shape to help promote plug-and-play compatibility between individual components.

Component software has inherent appeal. In an age of mass customization, who can argue against the value of prefabricated software parts? Yet, the compelling business case for components, the one that weaves together the highest value proposition for both component developers and customers, has not been fully apparent. The case exists, but to understand it requires that one appreciate the "requirements spectrum" that defines any vertical software market.

Curve of Commonality

If all of the various customer requirements could be identified for a given vertical software market, a graph could be constructed whose curve would show, in order of highest to lowest, the percentage of customers who share each of the identified requirements, as shown in Figure 13-1. The resulting "requirements spectrum" and its "curve of commonality" sets the stage for analysis of the value proposition for components.

On the left side of the curve are the requirements that are most shared. For example, in the vertical markets for sales force automation systems it is highly likely that 100 percent of the customers would require a contact management feature.

On the right side of the curve are the least shared requirements. At its furthest extent, the right side identifies requirements that are unique to individual customers. In the sales force automation example, a single customer might desire a specialized quotation generator that produces complex quotes based on a proprietary set of expert rules.

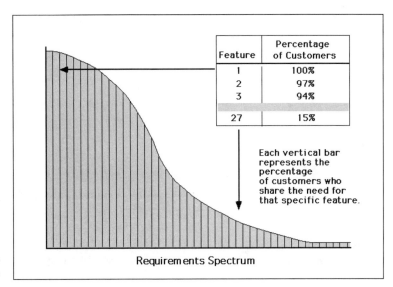

Figure 13-1.
Curve of commonality

A simplistic way of describing the spectrum would be to characterize the requirements on the left as "common" and the ones on the right as "different," as illustrated in Figure 13-2.

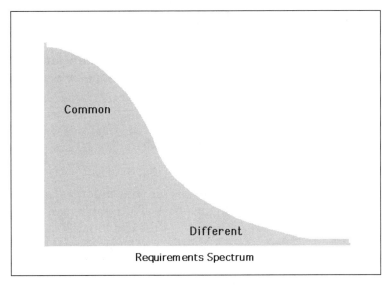

Figure 13-2.
Common to different

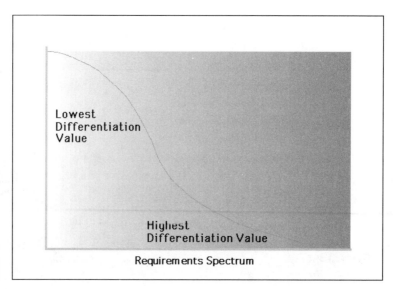

Figure 13-3.

Differentiation value gradient

Differentiation Value

The common requirements on the left of Figure 13-3 represent the lowest differentiation value to a customer. These are mainstream requirements that are shared with other customers in that market space.

The highest differentiation value goes to the requirements that are least in common—those on the far right that uniquely position a company within an industry and give it a major advantage in the marketplace.

Vertical Software Strategies

Historically, vertical software strategies have been based on positioning within this differentiation value gradient. This is illustrated in Figure 13-4. The suppliers of off-the-shelf, one-size-fits-all software try to meet the combination of common requirements necessary to hit the sweet spot for price and volume. Customers that require features that are well outside the mainstream won't be satisfied. Off-the-shelf software, by its nature, rarely progresses into the area of high differentiation value.

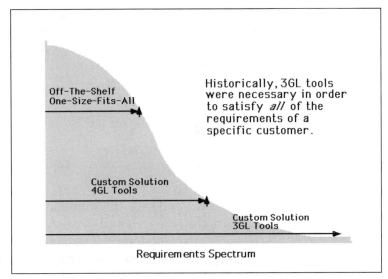

Historically, 3GL tools were necessary in order to satisfy *all* of the requirements of a specific customer.

Requirements Spectrum

Figure 13-4.
Historical software strategies

Fourth generation language (4GL) tools provide customers with the ability to move closer to a complete solution that will satisfy all of their requirements. However, the primary attraction of 4GL tools is their ease of custom application building, which comes at the expense of reduced performance and lower-level control over the technology. Eventually many customers hit these limitations as they attempt to stretch out the performance and functionality of 4GL applications to accommodate all of their requirements. In the end, they must often settle for less.

It has been the domain of third-generation languages (3GL) like C and C++ to deliver the complete spectrum of customer requirements. Unfortunately, programming in C and C++ is a complex undertaking that carries significant risks and disadvantages. The most frequently heard complaints regarding 3GL efforts are high cost and slow time-to-delivery. Of the two, the latter is often viewed as the highest risk, since business conditions often change so fast that many 3GL efforts become bogged down in the quicksand of change orders and are eventually abandoned. Customers who choose to fund a 3GL effort usually have very compelling, mission-critical requirements whose high business value justifies the risks involved.

The challenge to vertical software developers is how to give the customer all of what it wants without subjecting it to the significant risks associated with a totally custom, 3GL software development effort. It is precisely this challenge that component software is prepared to meet.

The Case for Components

A visit back to the curve of commonality shows the case for components is shown in Figure 13-5.

In most vertical markets, the common requirements on the left will support the research and development investment in prefabricated software components that can be reused within customer-specific projects. Component sets can be readily assembled, on a customer-by-customer basis, using the appropriate combination of universal, market-specific, industry-specific, and niche-specific components. With proper targeting, these component sets, or frameworks, should encompass up to 70 percent or more of the requirements for any customer-specific project. The remaining percentage will require custom code to meet a customer's unique and proprietary requirements, which in turn carry the strong business drivers necessary to justify a custom coding effort.

Figure 13-5.
Components plus custom code

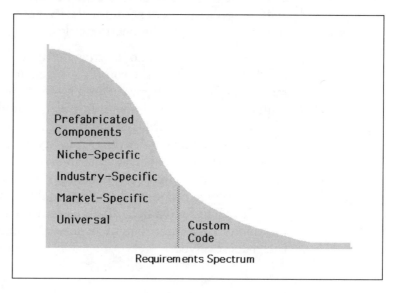

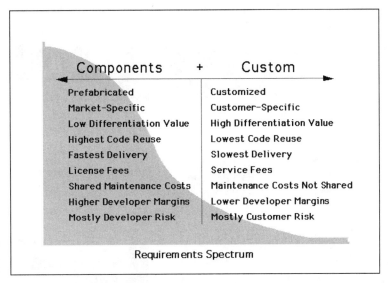

Figure 13-6.

*Major characteristics
of each side*

Figure 13-6 contrasts the major characteristics that describe the component and custom portions of the curve.

Combined, the two portions form a new value proposition that is compelling for both the developer and the customer of component-based software.

From the developer's standpoint, the opportunity to rapidly deliver high-value, one-size-fits-one solutions, yet still derive recurring license revenues and higher net margins through component reuse, is a highly attractive business proposition. Over time, a developer's market targeting, aggregate component library, customer-specific knowledge, and exclusive partnering relationships help form significant barriers to competition. Enlightened developers will use this attractive opportunity to invest in component factories and license the component output through several OEM channels, including their own integration and customization services, as illustrated in Figure 13-7.

Customers win big as well. Of highest value to customers is the opportunity to dramatically decrease time-to-delivery while improving the flexibility and reliability of tailored software that will meet all of their requirements. This includes the critical ability to keep up with rapidly changing business conditions. Lower

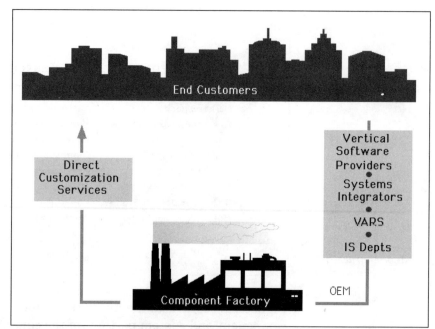

Figure 13-7.

Channels to end customers

overall costs, in the form of component license fees and reduced maintenance expenses, provide the icing on the cake.

Ideal Vertical Markets

It is important to note that not all vertical markets are ideal candidates for component-based software. In some markets, there is little need for differentiation between customers because most requirements are common, as shown in Figure 13-8. This type of requirements profile does not drive the need for various component combinations and is best suited for one-size-fits-all solutions that move sequentially through traditional upgrade versions.

The opposite profile is also problematic. In this type of market, there are not enough common requirements to promote financially viable levels of component reuse.

The ideal vertical markets for component-based software are ones in which there are many common and uncommon requirements. The common requirements promote volume reuse of components. The uncommon requirements, the ones with the greatest

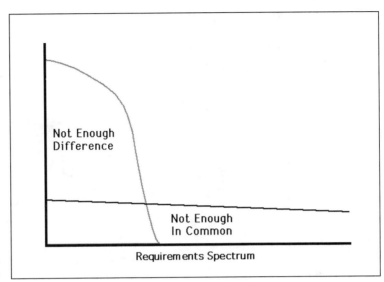

Figure 13-8.
Unattractive spectrums

differentiation value, promote various component combinations plus limited customization. Component-based strategies will work best in markets with this type of requirements profile.

Ideal Component Developer

It is also important to note that not all software development firms are qualified to design and build component-based, customer-specific solutions. Developers of off-the-shelf, one-size-fits-all software typically lack the customization experience and processes required to work successfully with individual customers. Conversely, most custom development firms lack the rigorous, 3GL development skills required to design and build reusable, high-performance software components. The ideal developer of component-based software has strong experience in both 3GL-level product development and customization work for individual customers.

Summary

There has been considerable industry debate about the value proposition for software components. Nearly everyone in the industry agrees that component reuse is the Holy Grail of

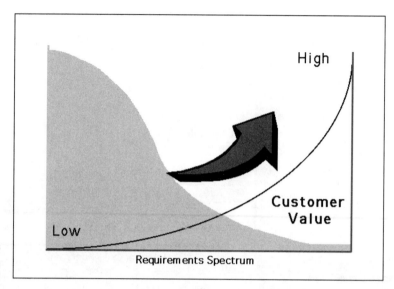

Figure 13-9.

Customer migration to highest value

software,but the financially viable route to volume reuse has not been clearly evident.

The highest value proposition resides in the domain of component-based software that can be readily customized to meet the uncommon and unique requirements of individual customers. Ultimately, demand for component-based software will explode as more and more customers realize its advantages and migrate their software strategies toward the high-value portion of the requirements spectrum, as shown in Figure 13-9.

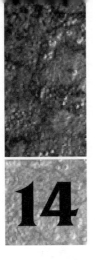

14

A Compelling Example: Apple's Cyberdog

This chapter gives you a look at the most compelling example of OpenDoc software to date: Apple's Cyberdog. Cyberdog is both an architecture and a set of OpenDoc part editors that provide access to Internet services. First shown in public at Apple's 1995 World Wide Developers Conference, Cyberdog provided such a strong example of what OpenDoc is about that it crystallized many developers' understanding of OpenDoc and the potential for component software, and it has inspired some to start work on their own OpenDoc software. In this chapter, you will first read how Cyberdog came about. Then you will see some of the user interface of the initial set of Cyberdog parts developed by Apple Computer, followed by an overview of the architecture and APIs for this extensible product.

Why Cyberdog?

The World Wide Web, based on the HyperText Transfer Protocol (HTTP), provides hypertext-like access to text, digital images, sound, movies, and other data types. The Internet grew at a rapid but steady pace until the introduction of the Web, when its growth rate became hyperbolic. Web addresses are now so common that they appear in advertisements on buses and newspaper articles. In fact, there are rumors that certain Web addresses have been written on the walls of public restrooms, but these rumors have not yet been verified. For better or for worse, the Web has caught the general public's attention like nothing else in the last decade.

The rapid rise in popularity of the Web and other Internet services has led to an explosion of software that provides access to one or more Internet services, both public domain and commercial. Additional services and data types are continually being introduced to the Internet. These trends have led to two types of Internet software. First, there are applications that provide access to a single type of Internet service, such as e-mail, Gopher, or FTP. Second, some vendors have attempted to deal with the rising number of services by creating "integrated" Internet access packages, which provide access to most Internet services in a single application. It seems that we all are living through a recapitulation of the rise of application suites and integrated packages, only this time it is not word processors and spreadsheets, but access to the Web, newsgroups, Gophers, and other services.

Apple was able, by fortuitous timing, to combine OpenDoc with the strong interest in the Internet to produce Cyberdog. Like the Internet applications, Cyberdog relies on industry standard protocols, such as HTTP, SMTP (Simple Mail Transfer Protocol), NNTP (Net News Transfer Protocol), and FTP (File Transfer Protocol). Unlike traditional Internet applications, Cyberdog uses OpenDoc as its foundation. This reduces the complexity of developing software to support Internet services. It also makes users' lives easier, since the user interfaces of each of the parts are similar and because there are common services available that work with all parts, such as a log (history) trail and a notebook for saving interesting net addresses. Further, users can add Internet access to any other OpenDoc part by dragging a Cyberdog part into it.

Developers will find Cyberdog of interest for several reasons. First, it provides an excellent example of how OpenDoc provides an architecture for developing what would have been a very complex application. Second, Apple has also announced its intention to make Cyberdog available on at least one other platform (Windows). Third, Cyberdog is extensible, so developers can create their own Cyberdog parts that work with other Internet services, provide even better access to Internet services for which Apple has developed a Cyberdog part, or work with other communications or networking services, including proprietary services.

Using Cyberdog

Before you look at what it is like to use Cyberdog, you need to learn some terminology (users of Cyberdog won't need to do this). This will enable you to relate the contents of this section with the following section, which provides an overview of how to develop Cyberdog parts.

A **CyberItem** points to network resources, such as a URL (Uniform Resource Locator). It knows how to "open" itself, for example, to look up a Web address, download the content of the address, and display a Web page.

A **CyberPart** is an OpenDoc part that displays the data associated with a CyberItem. Cyberdog comes with six CyberParts, which are used to access the following Internet services:

1. World Wide Web
2. FTP
3. Gopher
4. Electronic mail
5. Usenet news groups
6. Telnet

Cyberdog also comes with several other OpenDoc parts that are not CyberParts, but that provide useful services to the Cyber-Parts and the user:

1. Personal Notebooks
2. Log
3. Internet Connection facility (which allows users to connect to the Internet)
4. Other services (Preferences and so on)

Accessing the Internet

Figure 14-1 shows user access onto the Internet, in this case accessing a Web page. The user enters the URL and presses the Return key; the Web CyberPart then looks up the URL on the Internet, opens the Web page, and displays it for the user, as

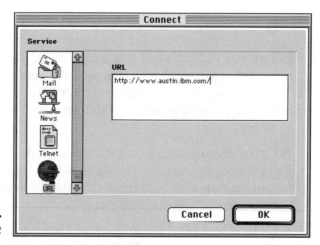

Figure 14-1.
Accessing the Internet

illustrated in Figure14-2. Users may also search for Internet addresses using a search capability, which is not illustrated here. The Web CyberPart is embedded in a navigation part, as are two of the other CyberParts: FTP and Gopher. The navigation part provides a standard interface for navigating the Internet. Notice

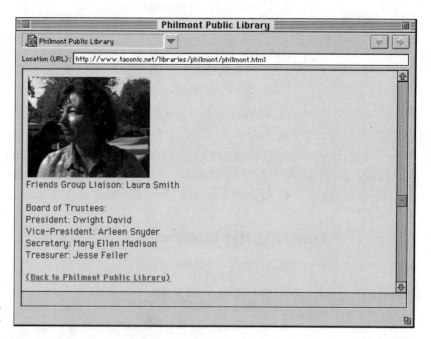

Figure 14-2.
The Web CyberPart

that the window contains a "control" banner at the top of the window that provides a set of navigation and other tools. Below it is a "location" banner that indicates the Internet location the user is visiting. The content is displayed in the middle of the window. Below the content is a field that displays the link name for the content under the current mouse position (shown only if the mouse is over another Web or Gopher link in the content area). Below that is a status banner.

To save the URL, the user drags it from the Web browser into a personal notebook, as shown in Figure 14-3. The user can create whatever categories make sense. Users can store any kind of network object in a notebook, including Web addresses, newsgroups, and FTP sites.

Users can manipulate items in notebooks in various ways. They can rearrange the order of items by dragging and dropping. They can move items from one notebook to another in the same way. And they can delete items by dragging them into the Trash in addition to the "standard" method of selecting the item and pressing the Delete key. Note how all these interface functionalities have been discussed previously—they are standard OpenDoc features.

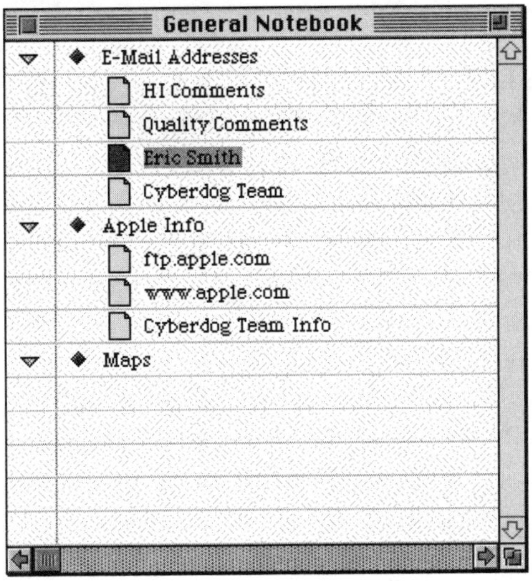

Figure 14-3.
A personal notebook

The FTP and Gopher browsers look quite similar, as shown in Figures 14-4 and 14-5. Each CyperPart allows users to specify their preferences, but these are not shown here. The Telnet part is shown in Figure 14-6.

Cyberdog also provides access to Internet e-mail using the SMTP and POP3 protocols to communicate with a mail server. The e-mail CyberPart provides the capabilities of supporting

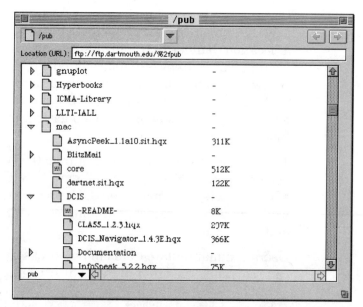

Figure 14-4.
The FTP browser

multiple mail servers. It also allows users to have multiple mail
trays for incoming and outgoing mail, as shown in Figure 14-7.
Users can create arbitrary mail trays. They also can specify rules
about how mail should be handled, such as automatically moving

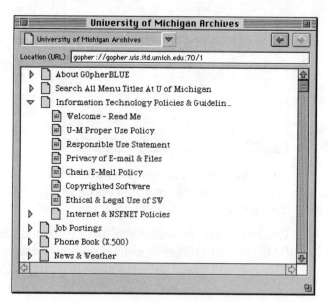

Figure 14-5.
The Gopher browser

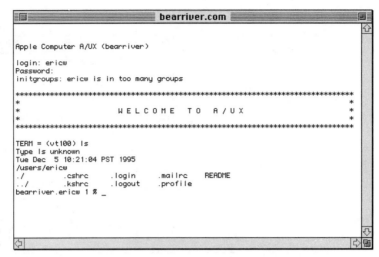

```
▤▤▤▤▤▤▤▤▤▤▤▤▤▤▤▤▤ bearriver.com ▤▤▤▤▤▤▤▤▤▤▤▤▤▤▤▤▤

Apple Computer A/UX (bearriver)

login: ericw
Password:
initgroups: ericw is in too many groups

***************************************************************************
*                                                                         *
*                    W E L C O M E   T O   A / U X                        *
*                                                                         *
***************************************************************************

TERM = (vt100) ls
Type ls unknown
Tue Dec  5 10:21:04 PST 1995
/users/ericw
./            .cshrc      .login      .mailrc     README
../           .kshrc      .logout     .profile
bearriver.ericw 1 %  _
```

Figure 14-6.
The Telnet browser

```
▤▤▤▤▤▤▤▤▤▤▤▤▤▤ Cyberdog Mailboxes ▤▤▤▤▤▤▤▤▤▤▤▤▤▤
        Subject              From              Date
▷ ▯ In Tray (eric@slip.net)
▷ ▯ In Tray (eric@slip.net@po...
▷ ▯ Trash
▷ ▯ Out Tray
```

Figure 14-7.
The Mail Trays window

mail items with a specific word into a specific mail tray. The mail handlers window is shown in Figure 14-8.

When the user views or creates an e-mail message, it appears in a window such as that shown in Figure 14-9. This is not your father's e-mail—you can embed arbitrary content, such as pictures, in an e-mail message because the e-mail CyberPart is MIME-compliant. Enclosures are simply dragged into the message wherever the user wants to place them.

Finally, there is a Usenet news CyberPart that provides access to the Usenet newsgroups. Figure 14-10 shows a list of news items from a newsgroup. Users can specify news handlers similar to the way in which they specify mail handlers, as shown in Figure 14-11. Figure 14-12 shows how the part displays a news item.

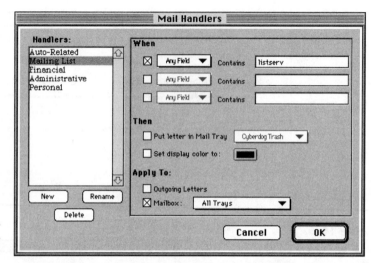

Figure 14-8.

The Mail Handlers window

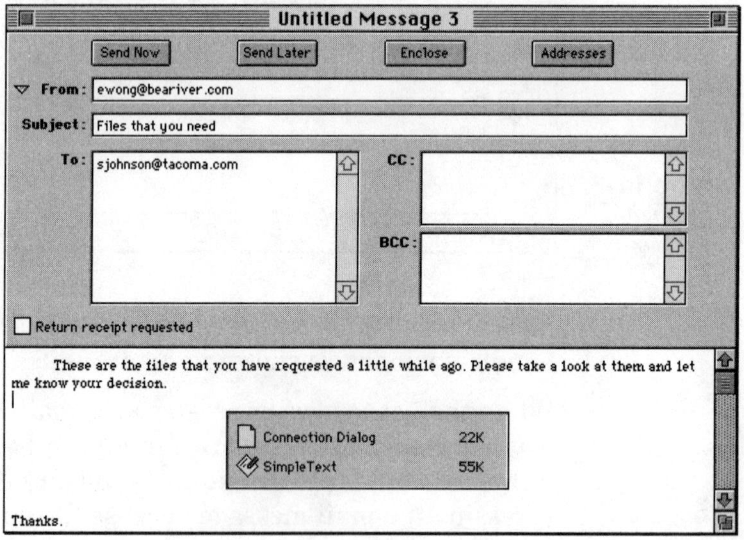

Figure 14-9.

Viewing an e-mail message

Another service common to all CyberParts is the Log shown in Figure 14-13. The Log is persistent between invocations of Cyberdog parts and contains the history of all Internet sites and services the user has visited. Users can view the Log's content sorted either chronologically or alphabetically.

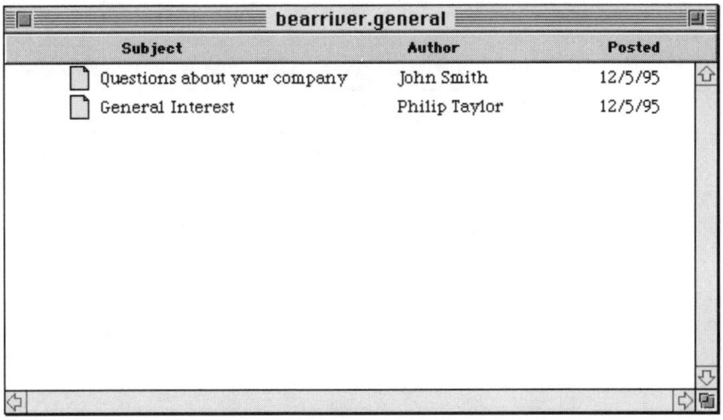

Figure 14-10.
A Usenet newsgroup

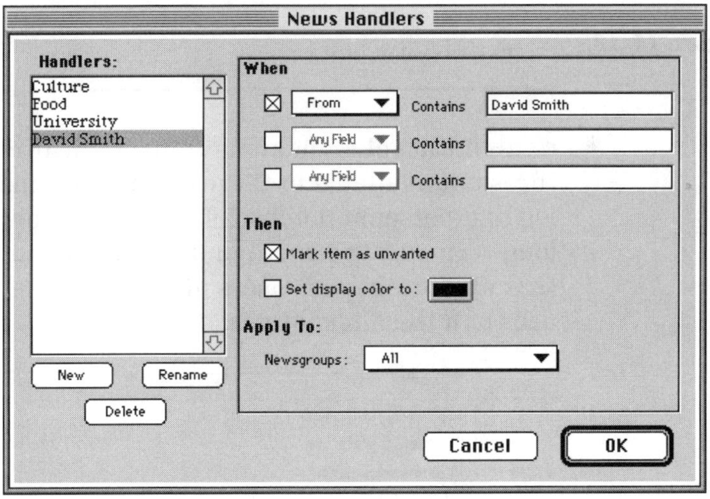

Figure 14-11.
The News Handler window

This brief look at CyberParts has given some examples of how they are used, but there are many other Cyberdog features that you have not yet seen. These include: "Pathfinder" support for less experienced users as well as support for viewing GIF, MPEG, and PICT images; for viewing QuickTime, QuickTime VR, and MPEG movies; for playing sounds; and for security and firewalls. Other features are reusable templates for e-mail (instead of just signatures) and dialup access.

These are all great features, but most, if not all, are available by using either one of the "integrated" Internet applications or a

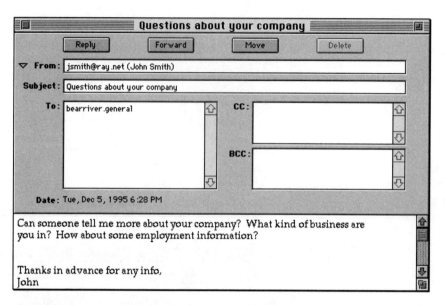

Figure 14-12.
Displaying a news item

combination of standalone Internet utilities. Some of the features not available in these other solutions are the integrated log and personal notebooks. Cyberdog's architecture makes its long-term enhancement and maintenance much easier than that of alternatives. Users also find that Cyberdog is easier to use than the alternatives.

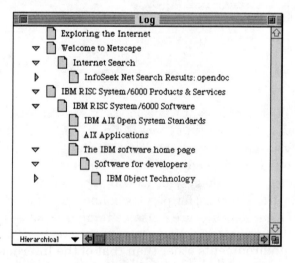

Figure 14-13.
The Log

Cyberdog not only provides consistent, easy access to most Internet services along with an integrated log and notebook capability. What is most interesting about it is that because CyberParts are OpenDoc parts, they can be embedded within any other OpenDoc part. Users can take advantage of CyberParts to do many things, including creating customized front-ends to the Internet. For example, they could create a custom browser that provides access to all of the Internet services that an organization (or its competitors) provide or a customer browser that provides access to content related to a topic, such as gardening or the ecology of deserts or space launches.

A **CyberButton** contains a CyberItem. When the button is pressed, the CyberItem is opened, revealing perhaps a newsgroup or a Web site or an FTP server. CyberButtons can be embedded in standard OpenDoc documents as shown in Figure 14-14.

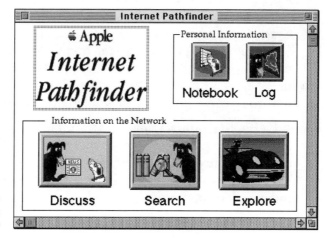

Figure 14-14.
Cyberdog Internet Pathfinder

Developing Cyberdog Part Editors

There are many opportunities available for you with Cyberdog. As you will see, taking advantage of them is very easy, since the architecture is quite simple.

Cyberdog Opportunities

Cyberdog provides an extensible architecture that can support environments other than that of the Internet. For example, you could write CyberParts that will support on-line services, bulletin board systems (BBSs), terminal emulation sessions, Novell Netware (IPX, NDS), and so on. The browsers and viewers you write can take advantage of Cyberdog services, such as the Log and personal notebooks.

Other opportunities are available in providing better Internet tools than those provided with Cyberdog as well as tools that extend Cyberdog to other Internet services, such as the latest Internet searching services. Also, you could create vertically focused versions of Cyberdog parts that provide added value to a specific set of customers.

Cyberdog Architectural Concepts

Cyberdog is primarily built upon four classes: CyberItem, CyberExtension, CyberStream, and CyberService. A **CyberItem** points to something out on a network; for example, a CyberItem might be a URL. CyberItem knows how to open itself, that is, how to create a part, and how to create a CyberStream.

A **CyberStream** retrieves a stream of bytes from a network location using a protocol such as HTTP or FTP. CyberStreams can be synchronous or asynchronous. They are an abstract superclass, so browsers and viewers can be written in a protocol-independent manner.

The **CyberPartExtension** class is a class which, when added to a Part, makes it "Dog-savvy." It is a new type of OpenDoc extension and, using this class, enables a part to make use of Cyberdog services such as the Log and the notebooks.

CyberService is a utility class that handles miscellaneous tasks, such as creating a CyberItem from a URL, setting up the Services menu, and handling the Connect dialog.

Developing a browser or viewer requires very little work beyond creating an OpenDoc part. Most of the network knowledge is handled for you when you use the Cyberdog classes. Cyberdog provides some interesting opportunities for developers to create communications and networking software.

Summary

This chapter gave you a look at Cyberdog, the first compelling example of OpenDoc. First, you saw how Cyberdog came about from the parallel arrivals of interest in the Internet and Open-Doc. Next, you saw some examples of how users can take advantage of Cyberdog. Finally, you studied the basic terminology relating to Cyberdog and the basic architectural units behind it.

Part IV

Developing OpenDoc Software and Solutions

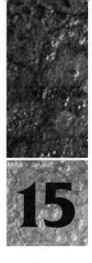

15

OpenDoc Interface Issues

This part of the book deals with specific OpenDoc implementation concerns. In this chapter, the issues related to interfaces are discussed; in Chapter 16, the OpenDoc Development Framework is described; and in Chapter 17, questions of conversion, integration, and planning are addressed.

When it comes to OpenDoc interface issues, there are several hard-and-fast rules:

1. Adhere to the guidelines—both the OpenDoc guidelines and platform-specific guidelines.
2. Make certain you know what your part is supposed to be and do.
3. Don't rely on anything outside your part.

Adhere to the Guidelines

There is something about most developers and designers that causes them to want (at least periodically) to ignore or flout interface guidelines. It may be the ignominy or frustration at being forced to use someone else's ideas. Or perhap the notion that the project at hand is so special and different from anything that has come before that it requires its own interface. Regardless, if a manager looks away for a moment, nonstandard windows, menus, buttons, and behavioral elements rear their ugly heads.

In OpenDoc, perhaps more than with other technologies and architectures, the interface guidelines must be treated as immutable. For all that OpenDoc is a natural reflection of the way people work, it is very complicated. Consider for a moment the processes involved in copying information from one part to another. (You may want to refer back to Chapter 9.) Whether to integrate information into intrinsic content, embed a part in another part, or create totally new encapsulating parts depends on a number of factors. Fortunately, with all of the feedback that is provided to the user, this process normally is not confusing. (The undo and redo stacks help further in this matter.)

But if the elemental feedback cues that OpenDoc provides are missing or modified, users may no longer know where they are or be able to anticipate the consequences of their actions. Therefore, you should always use all of these feedback cues to assist the user.

Fortunately, the plethora of feedback cues and other interface elements basically come for free when you build your parts using the OpenDoc Development Framework (ODF). As with all frameworks, you must guard against two dangers. First, too often developers do not trust the framework. They write too much code, either ignoring or not trusting the framework code that manages routine events and operations. Second, beware of "optimizing" or modifying the framework in order to make it work more efficiently. The places in a framework where you should be spending your development time are clearly identified. In the case of ODF, for example, you should be writing parts and their frames, not mucking around with, say, the event loop. It should be unnecessary to point out that projects usually do not have the luxury of spare time. The precious time devoted to a project should be directed properly—to the essential aspects of the work.

In some ways, it is a little upsetting that space needs to be devoted to this seemingly obvious point. Perhaps it is yet another symptom of the widespread computer illiteracy that abounds (that is, the inability for programmers or users to understand, analyze, and compare different software). If you,

Dear Reader, are one of those few gifted, self-confident, and well-balanced individuals who does not feel the need to reinvent the wheel of interface design, please accept the authors' humble apologies.

Know What Your Part Is Supposed to Be and Do

If you're not going to redesign OpenDoc's interface and your platform's look and feel, then you should be considering what your part is and what it should do.

Don't laugh. This elemental step in the design of OpenDoc parts is easy to skip. In the world of traditional applications (most of which have just grown like Topsy), the scope of an application's functionality is no longer clear. Does your word processor let you dither a three-dimensional graphics image? Can your spreadsheet let you edit desktop video? (The answer to both questions may be no, but there are word processing and spreadsheets applications that can do these things.)

OpenDoc parts encapsulate functionality and data in a way that people should consider natural. Designers (and users) will happily combine OpenDoc parts to construct the sorts of hybrid applications just mentioned. But each part should be focused on its own world. Focusing a part's functionality intensely will help you to make it *complete* and *reusable*. It is far better to have a word processing part that is the last word in text processing (and knows nothing about graphics, sound, or video), than to have parts that just sort of do most of the things that usually are needed in a certain domain.

Making a part complete within its scope doesn't mean making it big, you can define a scope or domain for a part that is quite small and focused. The important point when thinking about a part's design is to ensure that the scope for which it is complete is meaningful to people.

A part whose functionality is clear and complete is easier for people to choose—after all, it's the last word on X, not a mish-mash of things that may or may not be relevant. Also, it is more likely that your part can be reused, another important feature of OpenDoc.

OpenDoc parts may be developed as part of enterprise solutions as well as part of commercial software. These principles apply no less to enterprise solutions. Making your part the *ne plus ultra* in attendance tracking while leaving it blissfully ignorant of payroll issues will increase the likelihood of its—and your—success.

Don't Rely on Anything Outside of Your Part

It stands to reason that if your part is complete in and of itself, it should not rely on anything outside of itself. This doesn't mean that it should become a monster, in the great tradition of monster apps. A spell-checking part should be able to work well with a text-editing part. Your part's relying on things outside itself means it should not rely on a particular other part (e.g., spell-checking part ABC) or even that a type of part does exist. (You might want to spell check a spreadsheet.)

Defining the limits of your part—first to make certain it is complete and then to ensure it doesn't make unreasonable assumptions about other parts—makes it as useful as possible.

There is one notable exception to this rule. It is possible to create parts that have no user interface; they are activated by events sent from other parts. You may then design a part that contains only user interface and that can be used to drive the "faceless" parts. This allows you to plug a new interface into an OpenDoc solution, modifying not only the processing (by swapping parts) but also the way in which it all appears to the user. Research in this area is ongoing, and some remarkable products will likely appear shortly.

Summary

This chapter is mostly cautionary. OpenDoc has much richness in its interface and in the cues that it provides to users to help them perform the natural yet complicated processing involved with putting together and editing parts and their content. Hence, it is rarely necessary to make changes to the interface. Leave it alone. Focus on your part. Make it complete within its domain and make it independent of specific other parts. It should be able to work with other parts (possibly even sending and receiving messages from them). But if you concoct a melange of 17 parts each of which relies on the other, have you really improved on the monster app paradigm?

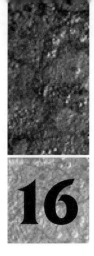

16

OpenDoc Development Framework

The simplicity of OpenDoc for the user is balanced by complexity for the developer who starts from scratch. Fortunately, tools exist (and more are being planned) to assist in the development process. The major tool is the OpenDoc Development Framework (ODF), a C++ framework that supports OpenDoc on the Mac OS, and Windows platforms.

This chapter provides an overview of ODF and its basic architecture. The principles of using ODF (such as what you have to override and what is different from other frameworks) are laid out, with examples from the ODFText Part Editor example which appears on the OpenDoc SDK.

This is not a complete overview of ODF—that requires a book all its own. What you should get from this chapter is a sense of ODF and what it can accomplish.

What, Another Framework?

It is always a surprise to discover that there are still people (some very bright and very talented) who question the use of frameworks. Some say their overhead is too great. Others resent being forced to do things the way the framework insists. Still others are very happy to use a framework, provided it's the one that they wrote four years ago. With OpenDoc, things have changed. Like a modern jet plane that is so sophisticated it must actually be flown by computers which are capable of making the instantaneous adjustments to ailerons and fins that these plans require, a sophisticated system like OpenDoc requires automated tools and frameworks for programming. You can do it without a framework and without even an object-oriented language, but you will waste an enormous amount of time.

In the chapters of Part II, you saw the pillars of OpenDoc's technical support: its basic technology, SOM, Bento, and OSA. With ODF, you normally do not deal with these directly. Although they are what makes OpenDoc happen, you can program in a remarkably "traditional" way within ODF. Here's an example.

MacApp DemoText TTEDocument::DoMenuCommand

ODF comes from a very distinguished heritage in which MacApp looms large. For over 10 years, MacApp has provided the base for many applications on the Mac OS. Many programmers have studied the code in the DemoText example, which is excerpted here.

```
void TTEDocument::DoMenuCommand(
    CommandNumber aCommandNumber)// override
{
    CStr255 aName;
    short menu;
    short item;
    TextStyle newStyle;
    switch (aCommandNumber)
    {
        case cSizeGrow:
        case cSizeShrink:
            if (aCommandNumber ==
                cSizeGrow)
                {
                newStyle.tsSize=
                    kRelSizeAmount;
```

```
                    fTextSpecs.theTextSize
                        += kRelSizeAmount;
                    }
                    else
                    {
                    newStyle.tsSize =
                        kRelSizeAmount;
                    fTextSpecs.theTextSize -=
                        kRelSizeAmount;
                    }
                this->PostCommand(
                    fTEView->
                        DoMakeStyleCommand
                        (newStyle,
                        cSizeChange,
                        doSize + addSize +
                        doToggle));
                    break;

        case cJustForceLeft:
        case cJustCenter:
        case cJustRight:
        case cJustSystem:
            this->DoJustChange
                (aCommandNumber);
            break;

        default:
            Inherited::DoMenuCommand
                (aCommandNumber);
            break;
        }
} // TTEDocument::DoMenuCommand
```

PowerPlant LDocument::ObeyCommand Method

Deep in the heart of the PowerPlant framework, a similar method lives:

```
Boolean
LDocument::ObeyCommand(
    CommandT inCommand,
    void     *ioParam)
{
    Boolean      cmdHandled = true;

    switch (inCommand) {

        case cmd_Close:
            AttemptClose(true);
            break;

        case cmd_Save:
            if (mIsSpecified) {
                SendSelfAE(kAECoreSuite,
                    kAESave, false);
                DoSave();
                break;
            }
            // else *fall thru*, saving an
            // unspecified document is the
            // same as "SaveAs"

        case cmd_SaveAs: {
            FSSpec   fileSpec;
            AskSaveAs(fileSpec, true);
            break;
        }
```

```
case cmd_PrintOne:
    if (mPrintRecordH == nil) {
        mPrintRecordH =
            UPrintingMgr::
            CreatePrintRecord();
    }

    if (mPrintRecordH != nil) {
        (**mPrintRecordH).
            prJob.iFstPage = 1;
        (**mPrintRecordH).
            prJob.iLstPage =
            max_Pages;
        (**mPrintRecordH).
            prJob.iCopies = 1;
        SendSelfAE(
            kCoreEventClass,
            kAEPrint,
            false);
        DoPrint();

    } else {

        // ++ Couldn't allocate
        // print record
        // ++ User probably has
        //no printer selected in
        // Chooser
    }
    break;

default:
    cmdHandled = LCommander::
        ObeyCommand(
```

```
                                inCommand, ioParam);
                        break;
                }

        return cmdHandled;
}
```

ODF DoMenu

In ODF, a similar structure exists to handle menu events. The major difference that you will notice between ODF and the previous frameworks is that the scope of responsibility for each DoMenu method is much smaller. This reflects not only ODF's structure but also that of OpenDoc: everything is much smaller in OpenDoc. Instead of applications and catch-all documents processing events, the light-weight OpenDoc parts and their frames do their specialized work. Here is the CTextFrame DoMenu method from the ODF Text Editor example.

```
FW_Boolean CTextFrame::DoMenu(
    Environment* ev,
  ❶ const FW_CMenuEvent& theMenuEvent)
{

  ❶ ODMenuID menuId =
        HiWord(((FW_CMenuEvent &) theMenuEvent).
            GetPlatformEvent()->message);
    MenuHandle menu = ::GetMenuHandle(menuId);

    switch (menuId)
    {
        case CTextPart::kFontMenu:
            {
                Str255 fontName;

                ODFacet* facet = this->
                    GetActiveFacet(ev);
                FW_ASSERT(facet);
```

```
               FW_CFacetContext fc(
                   ev, facet);
               CTextDrawInitiator di(
                   ev, fc, this);

           ❶ ODMenuItemID itemId =
                   (ODMenuItemID)
                   (theMenuEvent.GetCommandID(ev)
                   - kFirstFontFaceID) + 1;
               ::GetMenuItemText(
                   menu, itemId, fontName);
               fTextPart->
                   SetEmbeddedRunFrame(this);
               fTextPart->
                   SetEmbeddedRunFacet(facet);
           ❷ fTextPart->
                   SetFont(ev, fontName);
           }
       break;

   case CTextPart::kSizeMenu:
       {
               ODFacet* facet =
                   this->GetActiveFacet(ev);
               FW_ASSERT(facet);

               FW_CFacetContext fc(ev, facet);
               CTextDrawInitiator di(ev, fc, this);

           ❶ ODMenuItemID itemId =
                   (ODMenuItemID)
                   (theMenuEvent.GetCommandID(ev) -
                   kFirstFontSizeID) + 1;
               fTextPart->
```

```
                    SetEmbeddedRunFrame(this);
          fTextPart->
                    SetEmbeddedRunFacet(facet);
        ❷ fTextPart->
                    SetFontSize(
                        ev,
                        gFontSizeTable[itemId - 1].
                        fFontSize);
          }
          break;

      default:
          return
              FW_CEmbeddingFrame::DoMenu(
                  ev, theMenuEvent);
      }

      return TRUE;
}
```

Despite the similarities, there are a few differences in style and substance that are worth noting. In the two previous examples, a command number was passed into the method. In ODF, the entire menu event is passed in, and is parsed as necessary to find a specific menu and command (see the lines marked ❶ to follow this). (It's necessary to find the menu because the font and font size menus are built dynamically at runtime.) At the lines marked ❷, you can see the commands actually being dispatched to the part for processing. Since the data belongs to the part itself (while the frame displays it), this is a reasonable division of labor.

In the inherited DoMenu method of the ODF frame itself, you can see additional menu processing:

```
FW_Boolean FW_CFrame::DoMenu(
    Environment* ev,
    const FW_CMenuEvent& theMenuEvent)
{
```

```
FW_Boolean result = TRUE;
FW_CEditCommand* cmd;
❶ ODCommandID commandID =
        theMenuEvent.GetCommandID(ev);

switch (commandID)
{
    case kODCommandViewAsWin:
        ❷ fPresentation->ViewInWindow(ev, this);
        break;

    case kODCommandCut:
    case kODCommandCopy:
    case kODCommandPaste:
    case kODCommandPasteAs:
    case kODCommandClear:
        ❸ cmd = this->
                NewEditCommand(ev, commandID);
        if (cmd)
            GetPart(ev)->
                    ExecuteCommand(ev, cmd);
        break;

    case kODCommandSelectAll:
        ❷ this->DoSelectAll(ev);
        break;

    default:
        result = FW_MEventHandler::DoMenu(
            ev, theMenuEvent);
}

return result;
}
```

Since this DoMenu method doesn't deal with the dynamic font and font size menus, the incoming menu event is translated simply to a command id at ❶. At ❷, you can see actions being dispatched directly by the frame. At ❸ you see the common paradigm where a command object its created and then sent off to do its work (and be undone or redone as necessary).

ODF General Architecture

One of the criticisms of existing frameworks is that they are too big and that the learning curve is too steep. The ODF architecture is designed to address those concerns. It also is designed to deal with cross-platform issues in a simple and straightforward way.

Layers and Subsystems

ODF consists of three architectural layers:

1. Parts Layer (supports OpenDoc parts and gadgets),
2. OS Layer (supports platform-specific features, menus, resources, events, and basic OpenDoc functionality), and
3. Foundation Layer (supports strings, memory, exceptions, and so on).

Each layer may rely on the layer beneath it but must have no knowledge of the layer above it. Thus the OS Layer doesn't know about parts. Among other things, this means that the bedrock core of ODF—the Foundation Layer—can serve as the basis for another framework that doesn't know about OpenDoc. (This is not hypothetical. It is in fact what has happened. ODF grew out of the Bedrock project that Apple and Symantec sponsored at one point to develop a cross-platform successor to MacApp.)

Within each layer, there are discrete architectural subsystems (the aforementioned exceptions, parts, and events represent a few). In addition to the rule that a layer cannot know anything about a layer above it, there is a rule that a subsystem may rely on another subsystem in the same layer, but that that relationship may not be reciprocal. Either A knows about B or B knows about A. They both can't know about one another. (This concept has been used by designers for years; one expert expressed it by saying, "Data is like water: it flows only one way.")

This structure makes the code more robust and easier to learn. It is also a very good model to use in structuring your own code. You need to be aware of the basic ODF architecture primarily for one reason: Don't break the design in your own code. Consider your part editor code to be a fourth layer that lives on top of the Parts Layer. Break it up into subsystems and preserve the principle of nonreciprocal awareness.

Foundation Methods and Defines

To make code as portable as possible, ODF declares its own types. It also has utility methods at the Foundation Layer to perform basic functions such as exception handling and memory management. These methods and definitions are very important. In many cases, you can happily write code that works perfectly well without them. However, should you decide to port your code to another platform (or to an environment where memory structures differ from your own), you will be up a creek without the proverbial paddle. Using the ODF types shields you from this. Here is part of the FWStdDef.h file showing some of the ODF types and their implementation for the Mac OS and Windows platforms.

```
typedef     unsigned char      FW_Boolean;

typedef     unsigned short     FW_ResourceId;

typedef     unsigned short     FW_Milliseconds;

typedef     long               FW_Fixed;

typedef     unsigned long      FW_TypeToken;

// ----- Macintosh -----

#ifdef FW_BUILD_MAC

typedef     char**             FW_PlatformHandle;

typedef     unsigned long      FW_ResourceType;
```

```
typedef          FSSpec*                 FW_Instance;

typedef          double_t                FW_Double;

typedef          Rect                    FW_PlatformRect;
typedef          Point                   FW_PlatformPoint;
typedef          short                   FW_PlatformCoordinate;

#endif

// ----- Windows -----

#ifdef FW_BUILD_WIN

typedef          HANDLE                  FW_PlatformHandle;

typedef          unsigned short          FW_ResourceType;

typedef          HINSTANCE               FW_Instance;

typedef          RECT                    FW_PlatformRect;
typedef          POINT                   FW_PlatformPoint;

typedef          long double             FW_Double;

#ifdef FW_BUILD_WIN32
typedef          long                    FW_PlatformCoordinate;
#endif
#ifdef FW_BUILD_WIN16
typedef          int                     FW_PlatformCoordinate;
#endif
```

This code in the Foundation Layer goes both ways. If you suspect (correctly) that ODF probably overrides the platform-specific GlobalSize or GetPtrSize functions that you use when you write directly to the platform API, do a search on them. You'll turn up FW_PrimitiveGetBlockSize, which is what you should use.

```
size_t FW_FUNC_ATTR FW_PrimitiveGetBlockSize
    (void* p)

{
#if FW_OPENDOC
    return MMBlockSize(p);
```

```
#elif defined(FW_BUILD_MAC)
    return ::GetPtrSize((Ptr) p);
#elif defined(FW_BUILD_WIN)
    return GlobalSize(GlobalPtrHandle(p));
#endif
}
```

Using ODF

While OpenDoc presents a new way of working, this novelty is managed to a large extent by automated tools for creating SOM files and by ODF. The design of OpenDoc parts and systems that rely on them is different from the design of traditional systems (as is the use of such parts and systems). However, once the design is complete (in this new environment), implementation of part editors can proceed using remarkably traditional practices, particularly with ODF and with the automated generators of SOM files.

ODF implements much of the OpenDoc interface. Like most frameworks, the ODF manages events, windows, and system resources. When your part is asked to draw itself, the focusing and environmental adjusting of coordinates, grafports, and so on has been taken care of for you. The "guts" of many of your ODF methods are the same as they would have been with other application frameworks—or indeed with much of the code you may have written 10 years ago without a framework.

Traditional Framework Features of ODF

While there are some OpenDoc-specific characteristics of these traditional framework functionalities, to a large extent you will probably feel like you are on familiar ground. If you are used to reading code (unfortunately, many programmers are not!), you should have little difficulty following the logic in these basic methods. When it comes to implementing your own part editors with ODF, following these models and the examples that ship with ODF will put you far along on the right track.

The code examples in this section are all drawn from the ODFText part editor example in ODF 1.0d9/OpenDoc DR3. Later versions modify the code somewhat, but the structure remains the same.

Menus

As with most frameworks (and indeed with most applications), you typically want your framework to be able to carry out three basic functions regarding menus:

1. Create menus, modifying the basic menu bar that the framework provides.
2. Enable and disable specific menu commands as the need arises.
3. Respond to menu events.

In the first case, ODF provides the FW_CPullDownMenu class, which you can instantiate, modify, and then add to the menu bar. The following code snippet from the Initialize method of the ODFText part editor demonstrates how this is done:

```
❶fFontMenu = new FW_CPullDownMenu(
     ev, FW_CString32("Font"));
❷FW_CFontIterator fonts;
FW_CIntlString fontName = fonts.First();
for (fLastFontFaceID = kFirstFontFaceID;
     fonts.IsNotComplete();
     fontName = fonts.Next(),
     fLastFontFaceID++)
     {
          ❸fFontMenu->AppendTextItem(
               ev,
               fontName,
               fLastFontFaceID);
     }
❹FW_CMenuBar* menuBar = GetMenuBar(ev);
menuBar->AdoptMenuLast(ev, fFontMenu);
```

At ❶, a new pull-down menu is instantiated. The only thing at all unusual about the call to the constructor is the first parameter—the ev parameter—which is always passed in to SOM methods to help with error handling. Typing "ev" quickly becomes a habit. With the built-in exception handling of ODF and OpenDoc, catching and throwing exceptions based on problems with ev is automatic in most cases. (Keen-eyed readers will also note that the embedded string "Font" for the menu name, strictly speaking, should not appear in the body of the code. Localizing code is much easier if interface element names are separated.)

The font iterator at ❷ is a utility class provided by ODF; it iterates through all fonts on the system. At ❸, you see a straightforward call to add the name of each font to the menu, and at ❹, you see this new menu added to theToolbar. This code is almost boring!

Enabling commands in menus is equally straightforward, as this excerpt shows.

```
FW_Boolean CTextPart::DoAdjustMenus(
    Environment* ev,
    FW_CMenuBar* menuBar,
❶   FW_Boolean hasMenuFocus,
❷   FW_Boolean isRoot)
{
❸   FW_Boolean doneHandling =
        FW_CPart::DoAdjustMenus(
            ev,
            menuBar,
            hasMenuFocus,
            isRoot);

    if (doneHandling || !hasMenuFocus)
        return doneHandling;

❹   menuBar->SetItemString(
        ev,
        kODCommandAbout,
        FW_CString32("About ODFText..."));
```

```
ODCommandID cmd;
FW_CDynamicString fontName, itemString;
short fontSize;

// ----- Check mark the font of
// the current selection.

Boolean haveFontName = GetFont(fontName);
for (cmd = kFirstFontFaceID;
    cmd <= fLastFontFaceID;
    cmd++)
{
    menuBar->GetItemString(
        ev,
        cmd,
        itemString);
    ❺if (haveFontName &&
        fontName == itemString)
        menuBar->EnableAndCheckCommand
            (ev, cmd, TRUE, TRUE);
    else
        menuBar->EnableAndCheckCommand
            (ev, cmd, TRUE, FALSE);
}

// ----- Edit Menu -----
❻menuBar->EnableCommand(ev,
    kODCommandSelectAll,
    fEditText->CountChars() > 0);

return FALSE;
}
```

In the method's header, you will find an OpenDoc-specific parameter, hasMenuFocus, at ❶. Remember that each OpenDoc part can request the focus for any system resources, including the menu bar. Although this parameter is part of the inherited call, you can blithely ignore it when you are setting up your menus. At ❷, you see the isRoot parameter. This is used by ODF to stop the adjusting of menus, normally when the last item in the target chain has been reached. (The target chain is discussed in the next section.) You need not use isRoot in your implementation.

Like MacApp and other frameworks, menus are set up from the most general event handler down to the most specific (i.e., the application adjusts menus before the document and the document adjusts them before the window). This lets the menus be fine-tuned as objects closer to the user inspect them. This backwards-walking is accomplished by calling the inherited method at the start of the method, as at ❸. A typical change of a menu command name is shown at ❹, and enabling and checking a command is shown at ❺. At ❻, you see a menu command that is conditionally enabled based on a contextual condition.

The last thing you need to be able to do with menus is to handle menu events. In the next section, all ODF event handling is presented.

Events

The management of events in any framework generally requires that the framework maintain a **target chain**, a list of the objects that are able to receive events at any time. Typically an active window is given a chance to respond to a mouse click or keystroke. If it doesn't respond, the document displayed in the window is given a chance. The application itself also may weigh in if the document doesn't respond. The maintenance of the target chain is one of the most important functions of a framework. As you can imagine, once ODF manages the target chain for you, much of what you might have feared with regard to code complexity on OpenDoc disappears.

Each event is presented to the members of the target chain in the appropriate order. One additional feature ODF provides is the ability to add event handlers to any other event handler (such as a part or frame). Normally, you override the CSimpleHandler class and incorporate a special functionality within it. You can then add the CSimpleHandler to a part; the handler will be offered a chance to process events when they are presented to the part.

All events are processed in the same way using the target chain and whatever handlers have been added to the basic elements of the chain. Following are some samples of event handling from the ODFText part editor example.

Once you have created and adjusted menus as described in the last section, you need to be able to respond to menu events, as in the following code.

```
FW_Boolean CTextPart::DoMenu(
    Environment* ev,
    const FW_CMenuEvent& theMenuEvent)
{
    switch (theMenuEvent.GetCommandID(ev))
    {
        case kODCommandAbout:
            {
            FW_CacquireCFMResourceAccess a;
            FW_About(FW_gInstance);
            }
            break;

        default:
            return FW_CPart::DoMenu(
                ev, theMenuEvent);
    }

    return true;
}
```

In addition to menu events, mouse-down events are presented by ODF to the appropriate objects. Here is the DoMouseDown method of CTextFrame (which displays the text for ODFText):

```
FW_Boolean CTextFrame::DoMouseDown(
    Environment* ev,
    const FW_CMouseEvent& theMouseEvent)
{
    ❶ODFacet* facet = theMouseEvent.GetFacet
        (ev);
    FW_CFacetContext fc(ev, facet);
    ❷CTextDrawInitiator di(ev, fc, this);

    ❸EventRecord localEvent =
        *((EventRecord *)
        ((FW_CmouseEvent&)
        theMouseEvent).GetPlatformEvent());

    FW_CRect sbBounds;

    ❹fTextPart->SetEmbeddedRunFrame(this);
    fTextPart->SetEmbeddedRunFacet(facet);
    fTextPart->SetEmbeddedRunEvent
        (&theMouseEvent);

    ❺TClickCommandInfo clickCommandInfo;
        (fTextPart->GetEditText())->
            Click(&localEvent,
            &clickCommandInfo,
            NULL, NULL);

    return TRUE;
}
```

Once you get involved in drawing and handling mouse events, you necessarily get somewhat deeper into the specifics of Open-Doc. Remember that facets are the runtime structures that are used to facilitate drawing and event handling. Without bothering very much about it, you can retrieve the facet from the event that is passed in ❶ and then pass it on to the constructor of

CtextDrawInitiator (❷). At ❸, you see a sample of the type of code that is found throughout ODF to handle cross-platform issues. At ❹, the part is set with the active frame and facet as well as the event. Finally, at ❺ the information is passed back to the part.

You may want to trace these methods using a browser to study the ODF code on the OpenDoc SDK. This section presents only a high-level summary.

Drawing

Even drawing, where you have to think about frames, facets, and parts, isn't intimidating when you use the ODF structure. Here is the Draw method for the CTextFrame. As in DoMouseDown, the OpenDoc-specific code is largely passed through as you write your content-specific drawing routines.

```
void CTextFrame::Draw(
    Environment *ev,
    ODFacet* odFacet,
    ODShape* invalidShape)
{
    ❶fTextPart->SetDrawingFlag(TRUE);

    ❷FW_CFacetContext fc(
        ev, odFacet, invalidShape);

    ❸FW_CRect invalidRect;
    invalidShape->GetBoundingBox(
        ev, &invalidRect);

    ❹FW_CRectShape::RenderRect(
        fc, invalidRect,
        FW_kFill, FW_kWhiteEraseInk);

    CTextDrawInitiator di(ev, fc, this);
```

```
fTextPart->SetEmbeddedRunFrame(this);

fTextPart->SetEmbeddedRunFacet(odFacet);

FW_SPlatformRect plfmRect =
    fc.ContentToCanvas(invalidRect);

(fTextPart->GetEditText())->Draw
    (&plfmRect, kNoDrawFlags);

❺fTextPart->SetDrawingFlag(false);
}
```

At ❶ and at ❺, you can see the setting and resetting of the part's drawing flag (so that it knows it is being drawn). At ❷, the facet passed in is simply passed on to the constructor of FW_CFacet-Context, which the CTextDrawInitiator will use later. Note that at ❸, there is standard code to get the area that needs to be redrawn from the invalidShape parameter that was passed in. Two items are of interest here. First, the basic Draw method can invalidate an area within any shape; the text-imaging software handles only rectangles. Second, note the use of the FW_Crect rather than a platform-specific rectangle type. Starting at ❹, ODF's drawing routines together with the Draw method of the Textension (the text engine used in this sample) are used to image the text. (These routines are fully documented in the ODF documentation. The point here is that they function in the same way as routines you have come to know and love.)

I/O

Lastly, ODF provides routines to perform standard input and output functions. OpenDoc documents use the container suite to store their properties and data. However, there are many cases where OpenDoc parts need to interact with traditional documents and applications. ODF provides methods that read and write to platform-specific files, as well as routines for managing storage units in the container suite.

The Internalize and Externalize methods of ODFText use a number of OpenDoc and ODF concepts that are described in the documentation. In addition to storage units, data streams and data sinks (locations to/from which data streams flow) are used to implement the functionality. Here is the ExternalizeContent method.

```
void CTextPart::ExternalizeContent(
    Environment* ev,
    ❶ODStorageUnit* storageUnit,
    FW_CCloneInfo* cloneInfo)

{

    ❷storageUnit->Focus(
        ev, kODPropContents,
        kODPosUndefined,
        CTextPart::kPartKind, 0,
        kODPosUndefined);
    storageUnit->Remove(ev);
    storageUnit->AddValue(
        ev, CTextPart::kPartKind);

    ❸FW_CStorageUnitSink sink(
        storageUnit, kODPropContents,
        CTextPart::kPartKind);
    CValueStream *stream = new CValueStream;
    stream->InitValueStream(&sink);

    ❹CTextensionIOSuite *ioSuite = new
        CTextensionIOSuite;
    ioSuite->ITextensionIOSuite(
        false, stream);

    gCurrentPart = this;
    fCloneInfo = cloneInfo;

    TOffsetRange range2Save(
        0, fEditText->CountChars());
```

```
OSErr err = fEditText->GetRangeIOSuite
    (&range2Save, ioSuite);

❺fCloneInfo = NULL;
gCurrentPart = NULL;

❺ioSuite->Free();
delete ioSuite;

❺stream->Free();
delete stream;
}
```

The storage unit is passed in at ❶. All of the processing described in Chapter 7 has been done for you. By the time this method is called by ODF, all you have to do is manage context-specific data.

The code at ❷ is the same code shown in Chapter 7. ODStorage units are OpenDoc objects. ODF is not involved in this section of code.

At ❸, a storage unit sink (this time an ODF object) is created. The sink is located in the storage unit and will contain the contents of the part (kODPropContents) in the specified property values. A stream for the property's value is then created and initialized to use the sink.

Starting at ❹, the data for this part is written out in its own format. Remember that the structure of data within a property container is solely the business of the part. As long as the corresponding code at ❹ and in the Internalize method are compatible, you can do anything you want.

And that (except for a few clean-up statements indicated at ❺) is all there is to it.

OpenDoc Features of ODF

When you develop a part editor, you must override FW_CPart for your part. If your part is to be drawn, you also must override FW_CFrame or FW_CEmbeddingFrame (if your part can be embedded). Finally, you must subclass FW_SOMPart, whose role is simply to hand off control from SOM to your descendant of FW_CPart. (PartMaker automatically creates the SOM part for you so that you can pay attention to your part and its frame or frames.)

In practice, you will override many of the ODF objects, both those related directly to OpenDoc and those that provide utility functions. The best way to learn about ODF's wealth of code is to look at the examples. Remember that, as always with examples, the purpose of the examples is generally to demonstrate the functionality of the framework. Sometimes there are alternative ways of doing the same thing. Examples are good when they demonstrate this; production code is bad when it does this (that's called inconsistency). Also, remember that the examples will show you many of the things you *can* do. In reality, you will probably want to constrain your palette to fewer things.

FW CPart	CTextPart
	CTextPart
	~CTextPart
	Initialize
	NewFrame
	InternalizeContent
	ExternalizeContent
	DoAdjustMenus
	DoMenu
	Validate Presentation
	GetEditText
	SetFontSize
	GetFontSize
	SetFont
	GetFont
	SetSelectionJustification
	GetSelectionJustification
	GetAnyFacet
	HandleEmbedPart
	GetMainPresentation
	GetRulerPresentation
	IsDrawing
	SetDrawingFlag
	SetEmbeddedRunFrame
	GetEmbeddedRunFrame
	SetEmbeddedRunFacet
	GetEmbeddedRunFacet
	SetEmbeddedRunEvent
	GetEmbeddedRunEvent
	GetCloneInfo
	GetCurrentPart
	Initialize Textension
	CreateEdit Text
	StuffInTheText
	StuffInTheStyles

Figure 16-1.
Methods of CTextPart

In Figure 16-1, you can see the structure of the CTextPart, which is at the heart of the ODFText example. (Private methods are italicized.) Note that most of the methods have to do with the actual working of the part (SetFontSize, DoMenu, and so on). Eleven methods are one-line accessors.

The CTextFrame object is responsible for drawing the data and handling menu and mouse events. If your part is visible, you will always have at least one frame override. Many of the methods shown in Figure 16-2 are common to other text editing code.

In the figure, you can see the code that manages embedding as well as drag and drop. Fortunately, ODF packs a number of utility classes in its quiver. In Figure 16-3, you can

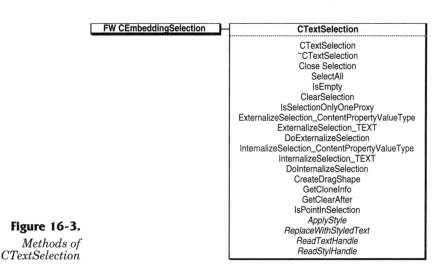

FW CEmbeddingFrame ─── CTextFrame

CTextFrame
~CTextFrame
DoCharKey
DoIdle
FrameShapeChanged
FocusStateChanged
DoMenu
DoAdjustMenus
Draw
DoMouseDown
AdjustCursor
EmbedSingleFrame
CreateGadgetLayout
AdjustGadgetLayout
NewDropTracker
IsDragHiliteDrawnInside
NewDropCommand
DoVirtualKeyDown
GetRulerFrame
GetFrameRect
ShowRuler
HideRuler
GrowFrame
SetFontSize

see the override of FW_EmbeddingSelection for ODFText. Most of the management of selection that was discussed in Chapter 5 is managed for you by ODF; you need write only your context-specific code.

Similarly, in Figure 16-4 you can see the override of FW_CDropTracker. ODF's implementation of drag and drop handles the interface issues as well as the general functionality (you still have to implement your specific data needs).

Figure 16-2.

Methods of CTextFrame

FW CEmbeddingSelection ─── CTextSelection

CTextSelection
~CTextSelection
Close Selection
SelectAll
IsEmpty
ClearSelection
IsSelectionOnlyOneProxy
ExternalizeSelection_ContentPropertyValueType
ExternalizeSelection_TEXT
DoExternalizeSelection
InternalizeSelection_ContentPropertyValueType
InternalizeSelection_TEXT
DoInternalizeSelection
CreateDragShape
GetCloneInfo
GetClearAfter
IsPointInSelection
ApplyStyle
ReplaceWithStyledText
ReadTextHandle
ReadStylHandle

Figure 16-3.

Methods of CTextSelection

FW CDropTracker ─── CTextDropTracker

CTextDropTracker
~CTextDropTracker
BeginTracking
ContinueTracking
EndTracking
GetCharOffset
DrawCaret
GetTextPart

Figure 16-4.

Methods of CTextDropTracker

Summary

This chapter can provide only an overview of ODF, sort of a taste of what you will find inside the framework. The most important points to remember are that it hides a very large amount of OpenDoc from you, particularly many of the aspects that differ from traditional applications you may have written.

The code snippets in this chapter are real and to a large extent could have come from PowerPlant, MacApp, MFC, or TCL. The OpenDoc-specific code (storage units, facets, frames, parts) largely requires that you understand basic OpenDoc concepts. The details of SOM, container suites, and the rest of OpenDoc are usually not needed for you to implement a part editor.

Because OpenDoc provides such benefits to users, and since with ODF you can implement part editors relatively easily (provided you are familiar with programming using an object-oriented framework), why shouldn't you just pull up your socks and start using OpenDoc?

Why not, indeed. There's one last point to consider. How will your OpenDoc parts interact with your existing applications? How do you get there from here?

The answer is simple: Turn the page. The next chapter covers integration and conversion.

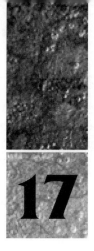

17

Moving to OpenDoc

How do you get there from here? We do not live in a world of OpenDoc parts, although conceivably in the future all (or most) software will be written as components. How do you make the transition? How do you start? You can consider three steps in the process:

1. Adoption of OpenDoc
2. Conversion of existing systems and applications to OpenDoc
3. Migration of an enterprise, organization, or individual to OpenDoc

These steps are basically the same whether you are the CEO of a Fortune 500 company or the CEO (and entire staff) of a corner grocery store.

Adoption

The first step is the decision to adopt OpenDoc. In some rare cases, you may be starting from scratch: your first computer, a brand new office, no preconceived notions, and no legacy systems. More often, people recognize that OpenDoc will provide value over the long term and that they should move toward it.

Whether you are in a company whose business is producing software or one whose business is something practical where software is only a tool, the decision to move to OpenDoc is likely to be taken seriously. OpenDoc does provide significant improvement in productivity and ease of use. Its built-in versioning mechanism for parts, its management of document drafts, and its preparations for documents that are integrated across a number of different machines on a network will clearly pay off in the long run.

In the short term, you may find it easier to stick with the tried and true. Making a decision to move to OpenDoc can be made long before you actually buy or create a single part. But having decided that this is the direction to go, you and your staff can keep their eyes open for OpenDoc articles. When new OpenDoc samples appear, play with them. See how other people use OpenDoc. Keep watching for the perfect place to bring OpenDoc into your organization.

Watch for toys and games made with OpenDoc! It's always difficult to convince senior management that "keeping up with technology" might require playing computer games—but sometimes it does.

And keep listening. As the world of OpenDoc unfolds, there will be new ways of distributing parts and interesting new channels for communication about parts. The Internet is sure to be a major player in all areas of software distribution in the next few years.

Part Merchant is an Internet-based OpenDoc software source that not only provides a convenient way of locating OpenDoc part editors and viewers but also allows you to automatically locate and download part editors which may be needed for a specific document that you have on your computer. Its concept of "software on demand" (or "just-in-time software") is sure to be a model for other businesses that arise in the component software world.

Conversion

OpenDoc is about people and their activities. In most organizations, many of those people are using traditional applications and many of those activities use non-OpenDoc software. As you saw in Chapter 16, ODF provides support for reading and writing to standard files. If you are supporting an in-house development effort, you need not convert an entire system to OpenDoc to take advantage of it. As you look for the perfect spots for OpenDoc to be used, you may find that on a temporary basis it is worthwhile to build (or buy) simple OpenDoc parts that ship data back and forth from traditional files or databases to OpenDoc parts. Then you can take advantage of the best of both worlds.

In developing or buying OpenDoc parts to use in custom solutions, learn to evaluate them in light of the standards discussed in this book. In particular, make certain the parts you use are as complete as possible. The existing world of overlapping monster applications is proof enough that complexity is an enemy of productivity. Wait to find (or develop) the part or set of parts that is the last word on a specific area of functionality. When you find it, put it in place with whatever bridges to existing applications that are necessary.

Migration

At a certain point, your hybrid environment will show signs of wear. It will be time to move everything to the world of OpenDoc. During your conversion process, you will likely have picked off the easiest and most appropriate places for OpenDoc to be used. The last steps may be the hardest, but don't give up.

The links and bridges you may have built in your conversion process will gradually be dismantled. While at first it will be obvious that you will want to keep data in native file formats, gradually the simplicity of OpenDoc's data storage mechanism will win you over. And all the while, of course, you should still be evaluating parts. There will be new ones, and new approaches to old ones. One of the nice features about OpenDoc is the independence of parts. You should not be presented with nightmare scenarios when you want to upgrade a small part of a system. Just replace the part concerned.

Summary

Once you decide to adopt OpenDoc, you start on the interesting adventure of analyzing what you do and deciding how and when to move the processes to OpenDoc parts. You may buy parts or develop them, but in either case you have an opportunity to reevaluate the work you and your company do. The initial part of the conversion process involves picking out the most obvious places to use OpenDoc—the ones with the least amount of work. Over time, you will start to address more complicated issues, building migratory bridges from existing systems and software to the new.

Any transition requires time and effort. The transition to Open-Doc is no exception. But since OpenDoc has been developed with a recognition of these realities, and because parts are replace-able with much less effort than entire systems require, your life should gradually get easier once you have made the commit-ment to move to OpenDoc.

As this book is being written, OpenDoc is being readied for dis-tribution to developers. There is no body of satisfied users shouting testimonials. But there is a growing sense among developers that OpenDoc may well be the way to continue to have innovation in the software industry. Old-timers regularly bemoan that the trade shows and conventions aren't as exciting as they once were. The fact is, the level of innovation in soft-ware is lower than it was a few years ago. The sheer difficulty of accomplishing anything within existing code bases is staggering (as is the difficulty of finding funding). OpenDoc promises not only a better and more productive way for people to carry out their activities. It also offers to developers the chance to once again focus on innovation and not have to worry about breaking a 1,000,000-line source code base.

Afterword

OpenDoc is a natural approach to providing the power of computers to people. OpenDoc (or something very like it) is where the computer industry must go if it is to fulfill its promise of improving productivity and empowering people. This is a promise that is far from fulfilled. The software that is being developed and sold today does little to improve productivity.

The major productivity gains that people and corporations attribute to computers and software are mostly created by communications, not by application software. The biggest bang for the buck comes from the network, not the desktop computer.

The difficulty of using software, its complexity, and the fragility of the customized environments that live on each person's computer desktop are substantial time-wasters. They are distractions from the tasks at hand, interrupting trains of thought like so many gnats. And things are not getting better. All developers on all platforms are working to make life easier, but the steady march of increasing complexity easily overtakes their improvements.

People still don't know how to talk about computers (the real scandal of computer illiteracy), and they are forced to rely on inconsistent and often inaccurate advice from friends, neighbors, consultants, and salespeople. (It is wise to remember that the computer salesperson in the mega-store was probably promoted from the microwave department last week.)

The experts in the field have a large stake in the way the world runs now. Billions of dollars have been spent developing the code used today. That's a substantial investment, and one can argue that at the time it was made it may well have been the wisest investment. But this system architecture (the particular closed design discussed in the Introduction) is wrong for tomorrow. Unfortunately, it will always be easier and cheaper to prepare a new version of an application (whether an in-house custom solution or a shrink-wrapped product) than to re-think and re-engineer the whole kit and caboodle. In justifying this short-term advantage, a number of people have jumped on OpenDoc and called it a pipe dream.

Well, take one moment to treat OpenDoc as a dream. Imagine a world with OpenDoc software. Think of the things that you do on your computer. How would they change in an OpenDoc world? Imagine leafing through one of the catalogues that crowd your mailbox and noticing a nifty new piece of functionality that you'd really love to have. Then consider the fact that you can have that functionality in a part editor without buying the $749 application that includes it (and that duplicates two other applications you already have).

Part editors that are very focused on a single functionality can be quite simple. Is it too wild to imagine a part editor with instructions for its use printed on a label on its diskette? (Note, that's instructions for *use*, not *installation*.)

Now think of things that you don't do on your computer because it's just easier to do them by hand or not to do them at all. How many of them could you do in an OpenDoc world?

Leave this dream aside, and return to reality. In particular, try to remember the last time you upgraded your operating system. How much time did that take? How many applications needed to be upgraded in order to take advantage of new system features—or even to run! The world that OpenDoc promises is focused on people and their activities; the world of computers today is focused on computers and their software. After the initial investment in a computer, much of the time, effort, and money later spent on it is on maintenance. The increments of functionality provided in upgrades to application and system software are balanced—and often over-weighed—by the costs and implications of the upgrades.

Much of the computer industry today is based on continual upgrades. From the user's point of view, however, a totally new application is more valuable, particularly in a new area (PageMaker when there were no other desktop publishing applications, Netscape in the Internet frenzy of the mid-1990s, or Visicalc on the original Apple computer when "spreadsheet" was a new word). The millions of dollars spent on upgrades are easy money for developers, but they buy precious little value for users.

Still, the cost of creating an application from scratch is astronomical. Few investors are willing to risk their money on such an endeavor when the opportunity to invest in the "easy money" upgrade business is at hand.

Paul Volcker's comment about the mergers and acquisitions of the late 1980s is relevant here. For all the enormous sums that changed hands and for all the work of lawyers, accountants, and others, he asked how much value was added to the economy from those events. (The answer, of course, is precious little.) In the computer world today, for all the money that changes hands, remarkably little real value is trickling down to users from the constant revising and upgrading of software.

But this is the way the computer world has evolved, you say. Perhaps, but those who have been in the industry for a long time (10 years or more) can remember when "computer" meant "mainframe." Things happen quickly in the computer world, particularly when people see the benefit of a new technology.

While who is or isn't on the OpenDoc bandwagon makes for interesting gossip around the corporate water cooler, it really isn't the key issue. The key issue is that the computer industry today is woefully inefficient, is not easily open to innovation and new endeavors, is much too labor-intensive and is populated by far too many people who are focused on short-range solutions to minor problems. The inertia and lack of imagination is frightening. "That's how it's done" has replaced the messianic rallying cries of the early days. (Of course, everyone was much younger then.)

Sort of reminds you of the time when the proverbial "two guys in a garage" were inventing personal computers while the staid, buttoned-down mainframe world looked the other way. It also has a bit of the flavor of the heady days in the 1960s when equally wide-eyed and visionary folk were wheeling teletypes and modems into corporate offices and connecting adventuresome executives to time-sharing mainframes, while the corporate brass worried about all those wires on the Aubusson carpet.

It's always hard to predict the future of technology, particularly computer technology. Will this or that platform be around in ten years? What about programming languages? What about network protocols? OpenDoc stands a good chance of being around for quite some time not only because it is such an open architecture where so many of the pieces can be replaced, but also because it is based on two critical things that *will* be around in ten years: people and their activities.

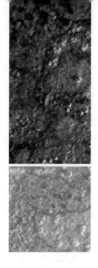

OpenDoc Resources

Component Integration Laboratories

Component Integration Laboratories is the nonprofit consortium of companies that support OpenDoc. Membership is open to anyone.

Contact Information

Component Integration Laboratories, Inc.
P.O. Box 61747
Sunnyvale, CA 94088-1747
Telephone: 408/864-0300
Fax: 408/864-0380

Electronic Access to CI Labs

info@cilabs.org	For general information.
cilabs@cilabs.org	To request an information packet or membership information.
http://www.cilabs.org/	The WWW home page. The Web pages on the CI Labs server contain information about CI Labs, technical information on OpenDoc, OpenDoc-related specifications, and pointers to other OpenDoc-related Web pages.

webmaster@cilabs.org   To report any problems accessing the
                              CI Labs Web pages.

Internet Mailing Lists

CI Labs maintains various mailing lists on OpenDoc topics, including the following:

CILABS-ANNOUNCE is a read-only list with announcements regarding CI Labs.

CILABS-INTEREST is for the nontechnical discussion of CI Labs's plans and charter.

OPENDOC-ANNOUNCE is a read-only list containing announcements of broad interest regarding OpenDoc.

OPENDOC-HI is for the discussion of OpenDoc human interface issues.

OPENDOC-INTEREST is for the discussion of OpenDoc.

ODF-INTEREST is for the discussion of the OpenDoc Development Framework and related topics.

BENTO-ANNOUNCE is a read-only list containing announcements of broad interest regarding Bento.

BENTO-INTEREST is for the discussion of Bento, the persistent object storage format used by OpenDoc.

How to Subscribe to a List

To subscribe to a list, send either of the following commands in the *first line*—NOT on the "Subject:" line!—of the body of an e-mail to listproc@cilabs.org:

subscribe <LIST-NAME> <Your full name>

For example: subscribe CILABS-INTEREST Al Gore .

ListProc requires only your name and will take your e-mail address from the header information. After listproc@cilabs.org processes your request, you will receive a welcome message that will give you more information on the list and information on other resources that might be available to you.

How to Unsubscribe

If you want to remove yourself from a list, send the following commands in the *first line*—NOT on the "Subject:" line!—of the body of an e-mail to listproc@cilabs.org:

unsubscribe LIST-NAME

For example: unsubscribe CILABS-INTEREST

If you are sending your unsubscribe request from the same account that you subscribed with, you will receive an acknowledgement from listproc@cilabs.org that you have been unsubscribed. If you unsubscribe from a different account, the list administrators will receive an unsubscribe approval request that may take a day or so to process. If you have trouble unsubscribing, you can send the command HELP to listproc@cilabs.org or send an e-mail to list-proc@cilabs.org to request that you be manually unsubscribed from any lists you do not want to belong to.

FTP Server

CI Labs maintains an FTP server that contains many technical documents on OpenDoc and related information. The server address is: ftp://ftp.cilabs.org/pub/.

IBM: Windows, OS/2, and AIX Platforms

IBM is the source for OpenDoc SDKs for Windows, OS/2, and AIX. IBM has also developed the Open Class Library, a C++ framework that can be used to develop OpenDoc part editors. The Open Class Library ships as part of the CSet++ product for OS/2 and AIX.

Contact information

IBM Corporation
Personal Software Products
11400 Burnett Road
Austin, TX 78758
Telephone (for product information): 800/IBM-3333

Electronic Access to IBM

opendoc@austin.ibm.com	To request SDKs.
http://www.software.ibm.com/objects/	WWW home page.
http://www.torolab.ibm.com/clubopendoc	

Apple Computer: Macintosh Platform

Apple is the source for the Macintosh implementation of Open-Doc as well as for the OpenDoc Development Framework, a cross-platform framework for Macintosh and Windows.

Contact Information

Apple Computer, Inc.
1 Infinite Loop
Cupertino, CA 95014
Telephone: 408/996-1010

Electronic Access to Apple Computer

opendoc@applelink.apple.com	To request the Macintosh OpenDoc SDK and the OpenDoc Development Framework.
http://www.opendoc.apple.com	WWW home page.

Caldera: Linux Platform

Caldera is the source for the Linux implementation of OpenDoc, as well as a Linux OpenDoc SDK. Caldera has also developed a CORBA-compliant Object Request Broker (ORB) that it has integrated with OpenDoc.

Contact Information

Caldera, Inc.
931 West Center Street
Provo, UT 84057
Telephone: 801/229-1675

Electronic Access to Caldera

http://www.caldera.com/   WWW home page.

Usenet News Groups

Developers can use this newsgroup for discussion of OpenDoc issues, news, and implementation:

comp.soft-sys.middleware.opendoc

Part Merchant

Part Merchant is an on-line source for OpenDoc software. Through its World Wide Web page, you can browse catalogs of part editors and order them on-line. Its PM Finder extension to OpenDoc modifies the user interface; when a part editor is required that is not located on the user's machine, PM Finder automatically opens an Internet connection and allows the user to download the appropriate part editor.

Contact Information

Kantara Development
Part Merchant
1125 W. Balboa Blvd.
Newport Beach, CA 92661
Telephone: 714/675-7327

Electronic Access to Part Merchant

info@partmerchant.com   email.

http://www.partmerchant.com/   WWW home page.

Index